REPORTING FROM RAMALLAH

Semiotext(e)
2571 W. Fifth Street
Los Angeles, CA 90057
www.semiotexte.org

Semiotext(e)
501 Philosophy Hall
Columbia University
New York, NY 10027

Photography: Alex Levac
Design: Hedi El Kholti

ISBN: 1-58435-019-9
Distributed by The MIT Press, Cambridge, Mass. and London, England
Printed in the United States of America

10 9 8 7 6 5 4 3 2

REPORTING FROM RAMALLAH

Amira Hass

edited and translated by Rachel Leah Jones

SEMIOTEXT(E) ACTIVE AGENTS SERIES

CONTENTS

FOREWORD

Some 500 articles and op-ed columns by Amira Hass were published in *Ha'aretz*—Israel's leading liberal daily—between 1997 and 2002 (not including news reports filed daily). Until September 2002, Hass served as *Ha'aretz*' chief West Bank and Gaza correspondent (between 1993 and 1997 she reported exclusively from Gaza, an experience about which she wrote a book titled *Drinking the Sea at Gaza*, originally published in Hebrew but since translated into several languages). Recently, she was released from the oft-grueling task of chasing breaking news and freed to focus on feature writing.

Hass is the first and only Jewish Israeli correspondent for a major Hebrew news outlet to live among the people about whom she reports. "I'm called 'a correspondent on Palestinian affairs'," she often says, "but it's more accurate to say that I'm an expert in Israeli occupation." As a resident of Ramallah, and Gaza before that, she not only observes the occupation but also lives it, an experience that invariably fosters identification but also engenders knowledge—the kind that only shifting one's position in the master-servant dialectic can bring to light.

Were it possible to publish all 500 articles and op-eds, the story told would be nearly complete: how the confiscation of land, the paving of bypass roads, and the expansion of settlements not only continued unabated during the "peace process" but accelerated as integral to Israel's "Oslo" logic. How by 1997, when our story begins, these unilateral Israeli "facts-on-the-ground" had already precluded the possibility of a viable final status agreement (in the form of an independent Palestinian state based on UN resolutions) originally set for 1999. How interim Palestinian self-rule in the form of the Palestinian Authority (PA) spawned political corruption, human and civil rights abuses, and economic inequities, in part due to Israeli dictates, in part due to negligent Palestinian leadership, but was always met with internal dissent and calls for reform and democratization. How Israel's ever-evolving policy of closure transformed the social, economic, and political landscape of Israel/Palestine so that after a decade of "separation" (in the form of an elaborate, demeaning pass system) closure became the most salient feature of Palestinian life, but also changed Israeli-Palestinian relations profoundly. How the Intifada, once it erupted in response to the above developments, fast deteriorated into an asymmetrical armed conflict between a handful of desperate, misguided militias and an army using unprecedented lethal force and escalatory tactics on largely civilian targets.

When Amira Hass tells this story, day in and day out—in "real time"—she does so with her own brand of impassioned indignation and sobriety. As Hass herself is apt to put it, she isn't objective, but she's fair. The role of the journalist, alibi de Hass, is to monitor power. This worldview is commensurate with the story she tells: not so much one of conflict between nations or religions, but of conflict between the haves and the have-nots (be they Israeli vs. Palestinian; Palestinian vs. Palestinian; or Israeli vs. Israeli).

Always grounding her version of events in fact, many of Hass' articles and columns are loaded with statistics. Few of these appear in this collection, however, as the numbers are constantly changing, usually for the worse: more dead, more injured, more unemployed, more units of land expropriated, less units of water provided, declining GNP, etc. Where figures do appear, the article or column addresses a trend deemed representative over time.

And what story does this collection of 37 selected writings tell? First, it is a chronological account. The publication date of each entry is inseparable from the entry itself. When Hass writes: "The conduct of Israeli negotiators is based, among other things, on the assumption that it is the Palestinians who will lose by rejecting an agreement. The Palestinians [however] are more accustomed than the Israelis to living poorly, and in uncertainty, and for longer periods of time. By no means is it obvious that Israel, the military power, will win the contest between the two peoples over who can endure more suffering, and display a greater patience," the fact that she does so on September 20, 2000—less than two months after the collapse of final status talks at Camp David and a mere nine days before the eruption of the second Intifada—is significant.

Second, it is representative, both of that which transpired in the said period, and of Hass' writing style. While not exhaustive, one can get an accurate, detailed, at times amusing, but more often heartbreaking picture of the later "Oslo" years (1997–1999) and the first two years of the second Intifada (2000–2002). Beginning with the violence of plenty and ending with plenty of violence, the gaps are easy enough to fill: colonization and dispossession, construction and destruction, impoverishment, confinement, desperation, vengeance, fear, hatred, and hope. One can also sense the different strategies Hass uses to address her readers (especially her Jewish-Israeli readers, whom she views as her primary target audience). In many articles she sets out to inform, explain, illuminate. In some op-eds she refutes, rebukes, but also pleads. Pleads for understanding. Pleads for sanity. Pleads for justice. Because Hass is first and foremost a humanist: invested in the wellbeing of both her community of origin and her host community. Reading through six years of her published writing, noting her prescience, one comes to think of Hass as Cassandra: the mortal blessed with the gift of prophecy but cursed with the burden of kinfolk who do not heed her warnings. (Though once, it was reported, an Israeli minister admitted that, "to his great dismay... the information provided by Amira Hass in *Ha'aretz* concerning some of the incidents in the territories has been more accurate than what he has been told by the IDF."— *Ha'aretz* 12/22/00).

Speaking truth to power, for Hass, is universal—a matter of integrity. Thus, no one is spared her criticism, not the Israeli authorities, not the Palestinian authorities, not even the *shabab*— the militant Palestinian youths whom she interviews in the second to last article (dated 11/13/02 but conducted before the final op-ed column in the collection was published on 10/9/02— hence the reversed order). It is this "exemplary courage and professionalism in working under pressure to deliver the truth," which has won her numerous awards, including UNESCO's Guillermo Camo World Press Freedom Prize for 2003.

Type her name into any Internet search engine and you will find that Hass' articles have been translated into numerous languages and reposted on countless websites worldwide. (Most of these are friendly, though some are not—if there is one thing Hass is well acquainted with it is hate mail). Since the second Intifada began, she has become something of an Israel/Palestine cult figure. As a Jewish-Israeli resident of an occupied Palestinian town, and the child of holocaust survivors who fought with the partisans and endured the ghettos and camps, she is assumed, and rightly so, to be a reliable source; a person with a unique subjectivity which, ironically, qualifies her for "objectivity."

Almost all of the articles and op-eds in this collection were translated into English by *Ha'aretz*. The paper boasts an "exposure rate" (as opposed to "circulation") of 300,000 people daily— a figure that presumably includes "hits" to their Hebrew and English websites in addition to readership of their Hebrew and English printed editions. While credible and coherent, these translations are at times more literal than literary (understandable given the constraints of translating news from one day to the next, and as is probably more often the case, one hour to the next). Thus, each of the selected translations was revised vis-à-vis its Hebrew original. The entries dated 4/20/97, 9/19/97, 4/30/00, and 12/20/01 were never published in English and therefore translated especially for this collection. The entry dated 06/02/02 was translated by Israeli peace activist Yehudith Keshet.

Special thanks to Amos Shocken for granting us permission to reprint these articles; to Ayelet Mitch of the *Ha'aretz* archives for her diligence and attentiveness; to Yael Lerer, Yigal Nizri, Lea Tsemel, Michel Warchawski, Philippe Bellaiche, and Simone Bitton for their helpful comments and logistical support; to Judith Jones, Linda Hawkins, Giancarlo Ambrosino, and Rolando Perez for their invaluable linguistic and stylistic input; to Agnes B. without whose generosity this project may never have been realized; and finally, to Sylvère Lotringer who, had he not been deeply moved by the poignancy of Hass' writing as a recipient, like many others, of forwarded articles on one of the many list-serves that sprang up with the second Intifada, this project may never have been conceived.

—Rachel Leah Jones, February 2003

PART ONE

_____

(1997–1999)

"When I lost my land, I lost my way of life"

April 20, 1997

Fourteen Palestinians in the West Bank and Gaza tried to kill themselves in March. Two succeeded. This was one statistic published in the monthly report of the Palestinian police that caught the attention of a young reporter for *al-Risala*, the official organ of the Islamic National Salvation Movement.

In past years such statistics were not compiled, making it hard to substantiate the claim that this figure points to a clear rise in the cases of attempted suicide among Palestinians. But the reporter's instincts, as well as those of others who took notice of the figure, are based on an insider's knowledge of their society, including exposure, from an early age, to the religious prohibition against suicide.

Most of those who tried to take their own lives were between the ages of 17 and 20. More than half were women. Anyone familiar with this society, certainly anyone living in it, does not need an expert opinion, and will not be satisfied with explanations tying each case to the individual's personal history. Attempted suicide—violently bringing harm to one's self—is an extreme expression of the despair, frustration, purposelessness, and overwhelming anger plaguing our neighboring community.

The political framework of stalled negotiations is too limited to explain the phenomenon. Deep disappointment was common even at the height of negotiations, when only a small Palestinian ruling and economic elite, and their cronies, were able to escape the continuing Israeli occupation and its capacity to determine peoples' lives and shrink their horizons.

The patriarchal framework that dictates such narrow margins for women's development offers a better explanation for the high proportion of females, who, it could be said, rebelled by taking their lives in their own hands. Better, but not good enough. Anyone who comes and goes between the two societies knows that the explanation lies with the Israeli-Palestinian conflict. However, anyone who wants to go beyond the provincial, reductive perspectives propagated by various intelligence services will seek an even broader, more universal explanation.

The minority of people who harm themselves, like the majority who do not, are victims of a violence often overlooked in the First World, unless its backlash hits them in the face (be it in the form of organized political protest, abductions, theft, or acts of terror). It is the violence of plenty. Were it not in the hands of the few, plenty wouldn't be plenty; it would be the rule, and nobody would take notice of it. But for the have-nots, plenty (physical and spiritual, e.g. food, space, esthetics, sanitation, cultural and educational institutions, employment opportunities, freedom of movement, leisure, etc.) embodies every possible historical form of discrimination and exploitation: the unequal division of labor and profit between the First and Third worlds, between north and south, between different ethnic groups, between classes, between rulers and ruled. Plenty draws the line between the worthy and the unworthy.

As far as the have-nots are concerned, plenty represents every possible violation of human rights, as stipulated by international law, which they haven't the power to enforce. First and foremost it embodies the violation of the basic principle of equality among people. Whoever lives with absence and experiences the insulting aggression of its incessant presence, naturally becomes a sociologist, a psychologist, a philosopher. Even without the attendant academic jargon. Ihab al-Ashkar, a Fatah activist and a member of the Unified National Leadership of the Intifada[1] in Gaza, used to say to his interrogators and jailors: "Do you know what your problem is, you Israelis? You think you are different from us, as if we aren't born, like you, after nine months in the womb."

At first, the Intifada inspired great hope in its proponents that it could stop the violence of plenty, as embodied by the Israeli occupation. That is, to convince the other side—through organized, political, popular civil unrest—that both peoples are worthy and equal. And that's exactly what should be worrying whoever is concerned for the future of both peoples living here: the loss of faith in the ability to enact change and resist the brutality of inequity. The distance from here to private and collective acts of despair is not great.

---

1. The first Intifada of 1987–1992.

September 19, 1997

Years ago, the children of Mevaseret Zion[1] used to go to Jericho, rent bikes, and ride around for fun. Their parents did not have money to buy them bicycles, relates Nahum Mu`alem, but their desire to "be like other children," and their resourcefulness, led them all the way down to this town below-sea-level. Two weeks ago, three of these children, today in their 30's, found refuge in Jericho.

A ring of unlocked bikes surrounds the Jericho Youth Center. The center itself attracts townspeople of all ages. What do they think of the group of Israelis whom the Palestinian Authority (PA) is hosting in a local hotel? The first, and expected response is: "Welcome!" But then someone reveals a hint of uneasiness: "Due to the closure, we can't feed our children." He wants to say: The PA has money to host the Israelis but not to help us out? Another searches for the real reason for the group's arrival, unable to conceive that there are Israelis who suffer at the hands of their own government: "Everybody knows that Israel takes care of its own."

It is tempting to see the entire affair as a ploy, both on the part of the refuge seekers and Yasser Arafat who received them with open arms. "Not so," insist the folk from Mevaseret. Immediately after their meeting with the Chairman (a week ago Thursday), "he could have called a press conference, but he didn't."

After receiving restraining orders banning them from Mevaseret Zion and the Jerusalem area as long as there are legal proceedings against them (they are accused of taking over an immigrant absorption center and holing up in it), they felt banished and decided to go as far away as possible, to Tiberias, to process the insult. Upon reaching the abandoned dwellings of the Aqabat Jaber Refugee Camp outside Jericho, the idea struck them. Sensational? Of course. But it doesn't diminish their truth.

Normative decency would regard their actions as illegal. But fact is, they only got public attention for their plight after occupying the Mevaseret immigrant absorption center three times, and being evacuated by a sizeable police force. All of their previous efforts—appealing to the local council, talking with their friends in the Likud ("We are Likudniks by birth"), lobbying ministers and other government officials—failed.

"After the establishment of the state," they reconstruct their history, "our parents were brought [mostly from Morocco] to the borderland, to this desolate place, Mevaseret Zion, to serve as a live fence." As they recall it, school was a degrading, castrating experience, which ultimately determined their futures. In recent years, Mevaseret has undergone gentrification, becoming a desirable suburb for politicians, military personnel, CEOs, doctors, and lawyers. Real estate prices have skyrocketed and along with them municipal taxes. Local residents, including people who have been working from the age of 15, and couples with two salaries, have discovered that they can no longer build a life for themselves in their native community. With the cancellation of the "Build Your Own Home" program (in accordance with the state comptroller's reasoning that it is a shame to "waste" such valuable land on public housing), they were told, both implicitly and explicitly, that they should seek housing elsewhere: in Beit Shemesh,[2] in the Negev, or in the nearby settlements. "Why should we head south to the Negev?" they asked as they holed up in the absorption center and pointed to their new, privileged neighbors, to whom they have given the general designation *Ashkenazim*.[3] In the same breath they mention MKs Tzahi Hanegbi and Yitzhak Mordechai (who lives in the nearby suburb of Moza).[4] "Let them go live in the Negev," they say. After all, the Likud—the self-proclaimed sentimental home of *Mizrahi* Jews—is the party that took Mevaseret off the "Build Your Own Home" program list.

The state spent a fortune on their forced evacuation; they calculate: hundreds of policemen and several helicopters. Experience has taught them that only "not-nice"[5] protest tactics can subvert the entrenched social logic, that moneyed people and other ruling elites are the only ones entitled to live in comfort. "We aren't asking for luxury, for three-story homes and private pools," they clarify.

Having been forced into taking drastic, violent measures, which the authorities were quick to dub "criminal," has led some of them to question Israeli claims regarding the conflict with the Palestinians. And some of the expelled, diehard Likudniks, have always, naturally, supported the establishment of a Palestinian state. "I never thought the occupation made any sense, as if we are superior—nobody is superior," said 'Oved Abutbul, who came to visit his friends in their Jericho hotel this past Saturday.

The 114 Mevaseret young couples in need of housing may be allotted a trailer park in their hometown. This is one of the "solutions" that would be considered a "victory." It is also possible that this struggle for social justice will once again be eclipsed by the ever dominant "security situation."

In any event, the Mevaseret homeless have written a new, alternative chapter in the historiography of this place: one whose parameters are not national but social, wherein two forms of dispossession are for once linked together.

———

1. Israeli suburb west of Jerusalem, population: 20,000.

2. Israeli town southwest of Jerusalem, population: 40,000.

3. Jews of European origin (except Balkan Jews).

4. Both Mizrahim—Jews of Asian, African, and Mediterranean origin.

5. Allusion to Golda Meir's reference to the Israeli Black Panther Movement as "not-nice."

July 15, 1998

The demolition contractor was most thorough, attested the Israelis who came to the village of `Anata on June 9th and saw the home of `Arabia and Salim Shawamreh and their six children being razed to the ground. Astride his bulldozer, the man sailed into the house attacking it wall by wall. Afterward, recounted Gila Swirsky of Bat Shalom,[1] he leveled the fruit trees in the back yard. The bulldozer also hit three water tanks positioned in the garden, and these in turn watered the uprooted trees.

The bulldozer operator asked to leave, but, as Jeff Halper of the Israeli Committee Against House Demolitions attested, a man named Micha, the Civil Administration representative supervising the work, said something to the operator and the latter returned to the house-that-was to crush a few more pieces of wall and fence. A battery of soldiers, border policemen, and Civil Administration officials prevented the agonized family and their neighbors from interfering in the demolition. A mere hour before, the family and their friends were still trying to object, clinging to the floor of the house and the garden. But under the cover of the soldiers' rifles and blows (the mother of the family was taken to the hospital), the contractor's hired hands (six or seven African foreign workers, noted Halper) were able to empty the house of its contents.

As the house was being demolished, young people threw stones at the faraway soldiers. The soldiers responded with tear gas and shooting. Three children were wounded, including Dia al-Atrash, 12 years old. He has since come out of critical condition, but has lost a kidney.

"This is the fifth house I've demolished today," the bulldozer operator told MK Naomi Chazan. Over the past two years, the Israeli authorities have destroyed an average of one Palestinian home every two days. In 1997, 249 Palestinian homes were demolished in the West Bank and Jerusalem, according to data compiled by Qanun (LAW), the Palestinian Society for the Protection of Human Rights and the Environment. From January 1st to July 25th of this year, 92 homes have been destroyed. During the term of the Labor-Meretz government, 268 homes were destroyed.[2] During the two years of the Likud government,[3] some 400 homes have been destroyed.

True, the homes were built without the required permits. "Illegal homes," officials call them. From 1997 through March 1998, 775 such illegal homes were built in Area C of the West Bank, which is under full Israeli security and civil control. The authorities were quick to issue 689 demolition orders in the same period. The rate of demolition has been rising in recent months, and now stands at one house per day on average. Twenty-two houses were destroyed over the last three weeks.

When the law is violated with such desperate audacity, one has to take a closer look at the legislative and executive authorities. Soviet Jews learned Hebrew despite prohibitions; until the

1960s, laws in the southern United States forbade blacks to ride at the front of the bus; nineteenth century statutes prohibited slaves from learning to read and write; in Ceausescu's Romania, listening to foreign radio stations was considered a serious crime. People have always broken laws that contradict the basic principles of justice and equality.

The Civil Administration and the Jerusalem municipality present each house as an individual crime: this one was not eligible for a building permit because it was constructed on agricultural lands, and this one was constructed next to a road that leads to a settlement, and a third structure (a school, for instance) was built outside the master plan. Thus, it is possible to sweep under the rug the fact that there has been a systematic policy, over many years, to restrict Palestinian building. One tactic is intolerable foot-dragging in granting building permits. Another tried and true method is refusal to increase the area defined in old master plans as permissible for building, despite natural growth. Since the land reserves of almost every Palestinian community are located in Area C, which makes up about 70% of the West Bank, Israel continues to control and manipulate the Palestinians' right to proper housing—all under the guise of the rule of law.

This is the same rule of law responsible for the 1967 demolition of the family homes of `Arabia and Salim, respectively; at the time they lived in the Mughrabi neighborhood of the Old City of Jerusalem, which was destroyed to clear a square in front of the Wailing Wall.

---

1. The Jerusalem Women's Action Center.

2. Accurate for period of September 1993–May 1996.

3. June 1996 until date of publication (July 1998).

January 6, 1999

Hundreds of thousands of Palestinians are criminals or potential criminals. They habitually break the law (by violating Israeli
military orders); or intend to, knowing they must. They live
with the knowledge that they will be caught. An unknown
number of Palestinians who were born in the Old City of
Jerusalem, East Jerusalem, or the villages that were annexed to
the city in 1967 live a few kilometers outside the current
boundaries of the municipality, yet continue to give their old
Jerusalem addresses to Israeli authorities, such as the Ministry
of the Interior and the National Insurance Institute. Should
they be considered deceitful people exploiting public funds?
Many other Palestinian Jerusalemites have added another floor
to their homes without obtaining a permit from the municipality, or after being denied one. Should they be considered real-
estate thieves moved by the lust for space? Every day tens of
thousands of West Bank residents cross the blurry green line,
entering Israel without the required permits. Should they be
considered infiltrators or trespassers?

A similar number of people risk their lives to go to Jerusalem,
which for years functioned as the economic, religious, medical,
and cultural center for Palestinians. They do so without entry
permits by car via villages and on foot by dodging the police and
army manning the checkpoints. The brave enter by taxi and pray
that the police officer or soldier will be too lazy to check all the
passengers' documents.

Thousands of West Bank residents live in houses whose construction was never permitted by the Civil Administration.
Thousands of Bedouin continue to resettle areas from which they
were expelled, until they are expelled again, because the rule of
law and order does not recognize the legitimacy of their way of
life. When they are caught herding in "forbidden" areas in the

Jordan Valley, their livestock is confiscated and held in lockup. Only payment releases the animals back to their owners. And nevertheless, the herders keep returning to the same grazing spots. Where else should they go—Ramallah?

Hundreds of Palestinian villagers, assisted by non-governmental organizations (NGOs) and the Palestinian Ministry of Agriculture, illegally seize paths leading to their fields before officials from the Israeli Civil Administration rush to forbid them to enact any changes in Area C lands. They also sow their fields, and the seedlings they plant are considered illegal. According to the records of Israel's law and order society, such territory is state land, designated for Jewish development only.

Gaza's incarcerated residents have fewer opportunities to violate the law, and nonetheless, it seems that hundreds of Gazans live in the West Bank without Israeli permission. Hundreds more, whose request for an exit permit to the West Bank has been denied, manage to get a permit in the framework of the Israeli imposed quota (300 individuals are allowed out of the Strip each day for "personal needs") in roundabout ways: usually through nepotism involving the Palestinian security apparatus. Others "disappear" from the buses that transport Gazan families to visit their relatives incarcerated in Israeli jails.

An entire army of Israeli law enforcers (Civil Administration officials, soldiers, police officers, military judges, National Insurance Institute inspectors, and informers) with a full array of "weapons" (computer data, aerial photographs, regular and temporary roadblocks) is charged with the task of tracking down, arresting, trying, and fining Palestinian criminals. Sometimes Israeli officials look the other way; for example, they turn a blind eye to the tens of thousands of Palestinian laborers who enter Israel illegally in order to work; or to the tens of thousands of Palestinians who, during the month of Ramadan, circumnavigate Israeli roadblocks to pray at the al-Aqsa Mosque in the Old City of Jerusalem, or to do their holiday shopping in the forbidden city. However, in most cases, Israeli officials strictly enforce the law.

They forbid Palestinians to build in Jerusalem and carry out demolition orders; they are quick to invalidate the Jerusalem identity cards of Palestinians who have the audacity to study or work abroad or who, because of crowded housing conditions, have been forced to take up residence in the al-Ram neighborhood just outside the city. Military judges impose prison sentences of six months or more on Gazans caught looking for work in Israel; the police catch hundreds of undocumented workers each week; senior officials in the Civil Administration reject requests submitted by Palestinians for building permits; Civil Administration inspectors dispatch helicopters to locate illegally planted seedlings or another house in violation of an ordinance; soldiers protect bulldozers as they demolish two bedrooms, a bathroom, and a kitchen constructed illegally by a family of seven. The same soldiers, or their comrades-in-arms, also protect the prefabricated structures that have been set up by Jewish settlers, without permission from the authorities. A Ministry of Interior official refuses to register a child on her mother's Jerusalem identity card because the father was born in the West Bank. The same official will register a Philadelphia or Odessa native who arrived in the country two days ago as an Israeli citizen with full human and civil rights.

A discriminatory and cruel system of laws is being rigidly enforced by thousands of Israelis who have never taken the time to consider what they would do were they on the other side. They prefer to see the Palestinians as a society of outlaws who must be punished. These Israelis do not bother to grapple with the old maxim that lawbreaking on such a massive scale says more about the lawmakers than it does about the lawbreakers.

March 31, 1999

In the afternoon hours, especially in the period preceding the Muslim holiday of Id al-Adha, the telephone rings every few minutes and becomes an increasingly oppressive device. People are calling to find out if there is anything new and one must respond to each and every inquiry politely, patiently and, above all, warmly with the statement that so far there is still no sign that the husband or son or father will be released from a prolonged stay behind bars. Deep in their hearts, without allowing their secret wish to find its way into words, the family members anxiously await the next call in hope that it will be the longed-for husband or brother notifying them that he is on his way home; that he has finally been released after being detained for a year and seven months without trial, without an indictment, without even a clearly defined charge.

Hopes build up in exhausting cycles, peaking every few weeks, before or after an out-of-the-ordinary event. In early March, 46 detained fathers and sons completed a 36-day hunger strike, but not before some of them had to be hospitalized in Nablus and only after the authorities promised to release all those against whom no indictments would be issued. Everyone assumed that in honor of Id al-Adha, which took place on March 27th this year, most, if not all, of the detainees would be freed. As soon as the hunger strike ended, the strikers' families stayed up, refusing to go to sleep. Every passing car brought the entire family to the window in excited anticipation. Similar hopes had been aroused before the end of Ramadan, which is marked by the holiday of Id al-Fitr. But these hopes were also dashed. "Liars!" children have begun shouting at relatives who promised that their much-awaited brother or father would be home for the holiday.

"Four holidays have come and gone, and our father has not come home," says the daughter of one detainee. The girl, whose father was imprisoned in an Israeli jail when she was born, reconstructs his arrest with a cynicism unusual for her age: "They said they were taking him away for five minutes, that's what the Palestinian security personnel told us when they knocked on the door and entered our home in the middle of the night. In the end, he will be released after five years." Other fathers, who were asked by security forces to come with them for "half an hour" or for a "short talk," have been detained in Jneid—a Palestinian prison west of Nablus once used by the Israelis—since September 1997. It is not difficult to find wardens who once sat in the same cells with those they now jail. One woman has a husband and a brother in detention, and another brother overseeing them.

Last Thursday a thick fog enveloped the ridges and valleys upon which the large city of Nablus is built. Nonetheless, the streets bore the normal commotion that precedes any holiday. The cars, shops, and billboards pierced the fog with cheerful beams of light, while children and parents on a mission to buy a new article of clothing, a toy, or festive pastries filled the streets and sidewalks in noisy gaiety.

The families of the detainees shared none of this joy. In the home of BA, they had planned to buy new shoes for the children who are growing so fast. It was only in the evening, between phone calls (which were either irritating or disappointing), that the family realized that they had forgotten all about their shopping plans. The children did not even protest. While the aroma of baking cookies wafted in from behind neighbors' doors, the women in the homes of the detained promised that they would do their baking "tomorrow." No one in these houses had any real desire to clean, tidy, or cook—as is customary before any holiday. "People wish me a happy holiday and I just start crying," BA admitted.

The detainees' families are not waiting passively for the release
of their loved ones. They run from one Palestinian official to
another, meet with members of the Palestinian Legislative
Council's Human Rights Committee, and then, with former
political prisoners from the Fatah movement. When the detainees
went on a hunger strike, their relatives held daring, impassioned
protests in Nablus. When the detainees challenged the legality of
their arrest in a petition to the Palestinian High Court of Justice
with the help of Qanun (LAW), the Palestinian Society for the
Protection of Human Rights and the Environment, it was the
women who came to testify before justices Sami Sarsur, Zuheir
Khalil, and Ayman Nasser al-Din. Covered with white veils over
dark robes that frequently conceal a pair of jeans, these two-dozen
women stood out in the gray corridors of the Ramallah court-
house. On several occasions they also filled the courtyard of the
Palestinian Legislative Council (PLC) building, where time and
again the legislators have condemned the arbitrary, illegal deten-
tions carried out on orders from the executive branch[1] and have
passed resolutions endorsing the release of those "against whom
no indictment has been issued."

Unlike comparable petitions to the Israeli High Court of
Justice, and unlike similar demonstrations demanding the release
of Palestinian political prisoners held by Israel, their activities do
not receive attention in the Palestinian press. The hunger strikes
(the latest one being the fourth since September 1997) are only
reported on when the authorities gleefully announce that they
have been broken. Every hunger strike has ended with the
promise of release, and renewed disappointment. People have
stopped counting the number of times the justices on the bench
of the Palestinian High Court have ordered the release of persons
detained without a warrant who have been behind bars for a year
or two or even three. According to various estimates, there are
some 200 political detainees, that is, individuals identified with

the Islamic opposition movements who are held without due process in Palestinian jails.

Faced with no other option, and basing their decisions on laws that clearly forbid arbitrary arrests, the Palestinian High Court justices invariably order the "release within ten days" or two weeks of illegally detained persons, if the Palestinian authorities cannot produce a satisfactory explanation for their continued detention. The executive branch does not bother to respond, and there is no agency capable of enforcing the decisions of the judiciary.

The detainees' wives and mothers relate how, in one of their demonstrations before the PLC building, they requested to meet with Minister of Justice Freih Abu Meddein. "He fled from us as if we were the plague," they recall in laughter mixed with sorrow. "Everyone knows that he is not the one who decides." And everyone knows who in fact does make the decisions. Some of the detainees' wives and children have met with Yasser Arafat. The meeting was brief, lasting no more than five minutes, but long enough for the children to discover that on television he looks much larger than he does in real life. "We tried to explain the situation," the women said, "but he just kept on saying, '*Inshallah*[2], I will get them out.'"

Indeed, during Ramadan Arafat did order the release of four detainees who were on the original list submitted to the High Court. "These four had connections," one of the women commented. Last Saturday, the first day of Id al-Adha, Arafat ordered the release of another nine, but only after the families of all the detainees had gathered in the prison courtyard, declaring a sit-down strike "until our men come home." The release tactics are clear: do everything possible to sever the link between the release and the unequivocal instructions of the judiciary, and undermine the feeling of solidarity uniting the detainees and their families.

Still, many detainees remain in prison, and their families' schedules are structured around the days when visits are permitted: Mondays and Fridays. The night before a visit the children write letters and draw pictures for their fathers. On Fridays, "when everyone else is still sleeping," and on Mondays immediately after school, "when all the other kids go to play or do homework," they head for the prison. They meet in the yard if it is not raining, or in the cells, which hold four prisoners each, if it is. Over-crowding precludes the possibility that a couple converse intimately. The children complain that Daddy has no time for them: all the visitors come to greet him, or consult with him, and they don't even get five minutes in which to play or talk. The children have informed their fathers that after they are released they will build them mosques near the house, so they won't have to venture far to pray.

Some of the detainees' children say with characteristic directness and a big smile—indicating the absurdity of their statement—that they prefer Israeli to Palestinian jails. True, the trip to the Israeli jail was exhausting, and visits were shorter and less frequent than they are in the Palestinian prisons, but at least the date of release from detention was more or less known. "In the Palestinian prison we can touch one another, the kids can sit on his lap. The prison is nearby. For a few hours we live the illusion of proximity and normalcy, and then we are torn apart once again and head home into uncertainty—an emptiness that not even an abstract date can fill," laments one detainee's wife.

During the visits, the children plan the great escape: they'll dig a tunnel, steal the guard's gun, hide the father in their clothes, and sneak him past the gate. When the holidays near they buy plastic handcuffs and play prisoners and wardens. Or else they stage mock demonstrations. "We are planning to arrest the Jews who arrested Dad," explains one girl, and immediately corrects herself "I mean the *Sulta*, the PA police."

31

One mother relays, "some guards overhear them speaking like that and get angry. They tell us, 'Is that what you teach your children?' And I retort that I don't have the time to sit them down and teach them anything." All the women function as both mother and father, only "Daddy took us to restaurants, to the amusement park, and Mommy only takes us to jail," the children complain. Some women teach school, others manage the stores their husbands opened, and their daughters run the house. As prisoners' wives during the Intifada,[3] they assumed an independent attitude that surpasses that of most Palestinian women, let alone traditional ones. "I am happy to take responsibility," says BA, "but not all the responsibility," and explains how much her husband helped her with the housework.

One difficulty they face is discussed with tight-lipped brevity: when the men were detained in Israeli jails, the entire society stood behind them. Detention and arrest were experiences that touched every Palestinian household regardless of political affiliation. Detention in a Palestinian prison mutes the expression of solidarity. Those who disapprove of the arrests are afraid to speak out lest they be harmed, observe the detainees' families. Neighbors who work with the PA or its security apparatus greet them hurriedly in the stairwell or on the sidewalk, never asking after their detained neighbor. Other children at school ask with curiosity, maybe once or twice, "What's with your Dad?" and that's it. Most teachers, utter not a word. The detainees' children are not ostracized, but they do not receive the kind of love they used to get when their fathers were held in Israeli jails.

"Why was your father arrested?" the children are asked, and they offer a variety of responses. "For no reason," some say. "Because he prays," suggest others. "Because he's Hamas," rules a third. The wife swears that he's "not involved in anything [military]." "How do you know?" "Because a woman senses what her partner is up to, and if he did do anything, then let them prosecute him for it." Some kids joke at the expense of the guards: "Dad was arrested for his own protection [from the Israelis or from Palestinian collaborators]," they repeat the excuses they hear from the prison authorities. Or: "He's not under arrest, he's our guest," a statement that led some of the women to inquire: "Then why don't you host us in your prison as well?"

Ironically, the detainees' families are being assisted by Palestinian human rights organizations set up during the direct Israeli occupation by leftist, secular groups. Most of Qanun's members are identified with the Palestinian People's Party, al-Damir, which supports prisoners' rights, is associated with the PFLP, and the Palestinian Center for Human Rights, which submits petitions on behalf of Gazan detainees, also has leftist roots. Traditionally, the Islamic groups have regarded the Left as political enemies, and shared opposition to the Oslo process has not reduced their core ideological and cultural differences.

Last week, the detainees treated their advocates to chocolate, for the bitterness of captivity was offset momentarily by sweet victory: The Islamic groups won by a landslide in last week's university student association elections in Gaza, Hebron, and Bir-Zeit—the former bastion of the PLO and the Left. "We are talking about basic human rights, not politics," explained an activist with one of the organizations that has taken up the unconditional struggle against the PA's policy of arbitrary arrests.

---

1. The Palestinian Authority.

2. Arabic for "God willing."

3. The first Intifada of 1987–1992.

October 5, 1999

Before 1967, residents of Abu Dis, a village of east of Jerusalem, "divided up the land between them. Each family had a bit of land. All together the village owned 50 square kilometers of land, which extended all the way to the Dead Sea. Almost all the land was in use, either as pastures or for growing wheat and barley." This is how Salah Abu Hilal, the mayor of Abu Dis, remembers things, and this is how he is quoted in a recent report by B'Tselem[1] titled "On The Way To Annexation: Human Rights Violations Resulting from the Establishment and Expansion of the Ma`aleh Adumim Settlement." The report was published last week.

Ma`aleh Adumim was founded as a "work camp" on the Jerusalem-Jericho highway in 1975. Initially, it was settled by the families of 25 workers at the industrial zone established on the site a year earlier. In 1979, the military commander of the West Bank ordered the establishment of a local council in the settlement. In October 1992, Ma`aleh Adumim became the first settlement in the occupied territories to be declared a city. Today, it has a population of about 25,000. In August 1994, 12,000 dunams[2] were annexed to Ma`aleh Adumim, bringing its total landmass to about 53,000 dunams. For the sake of comparison, Tel Aviv is about 50,553 dunams in size. The expansion plans completed in 1998 include residential, commercial, and industrial areas as well as hotels, cemeteries, parks, and sports complexes. At present, the city is waiting for the detailed plans to be submitted in order to commence building.

The area that is Ma`aleh Adumim came under its jurisdiction after having been declared "state lands" over the years. As far as the Palestinian community is concerned, and the residents of Abu Dis, `Anata, `Azariya, al-Tor, and `Isawiya in particular, the land, which they used to farm and herd, was theirs, and

34

served as a reserve for natural growth and expansion. The area also served members of the Jahalin tribe (who were expelled from the Negev in the early 1950s) along with the Sawahra tribe. "Now," says Abu Hilal, "there is not enough land for construction... people uproot trees and build in their stead." Abed al-Aziz Iyad, also of Abu Dis, relates: "Our family had some 3,000 dunams of agricultural land... I lost all the land... Except for my home, I have no land at all anymore. I still work the [expropriated] parcels which have been designated for the expansion of Ma`aleh Adumim. My children work elsewhere... My adult children still live at home because they have nowhere to build." Muhammad Zeidan, a resident of the village of `Anata, relates: "My whole family used to work together. We planted together, plowed together. We knew what it meant to work collectively. It strengthened our ties as a family and a village, because when we finished work on our plot, we would go to other people's land and help them... The expropriation of the land is the expropriation of our way of life. When I lost my land, I lost my way of life."

These are just a few of the testimonies gathered by B'Tselem's researchers, and footnoted in the report as "testimony" among other sources (legal, historical, etc.). But in the Civil Administration's response to the report, spokesman Captain Peter Lerner wrote: "The people who conducted the 'research' and the interviewees themselves are not professionals. They are not familiar with the professional history and legislation of the area, and therefore, most of their claims are based on faulty and misleading information."

The dismissal of B'Tselem's professionalism and the validity of the memories relayed by the original inhabitants of the area is not surprising. The Civil Administration was established as the civilian arm of the IDF, the branch of government responsible for "seeing to the needs of the locals." But over the years, various Civil Administration committees and departments have been instrumental to the implementation of land expropriation in the West Bank and Gaza. The Supreme Planning Council for Judea and Samaria, part of the Civil Administration, is party to the Ma`aleh Adumim expansion plan. It is made up exclusively of Israelis. The subcommittee in charge of appeals to the council, which in 1998 heard the objections to the plan of 66 Palestinian residents, is made up exclusively of Israelis, including a representative of the Ma`aleh Adumim municipality. The objections (which claimed that the annexed land is the only remaining land reserve for the villages) were, of course, rejected.

Following the rejection, the Palestinian residents, at the behest of their attorneys from the Jerusalem Center for Legal Aid and Human Rights, decided to petition the High Court of Justice with the help of Israeli attorney Avigdor Feldman. The petition, which will be heard tomorrow, asks the court to issue an injunction preventing the respondents (the commander of IDF forces in Judea and Samaria and the Supreme Planning Council in Judea and Samaria) from making any changes in the lands of the disputed area or from approving the detailed plans for the area until the final decision on the petition. The petition also presents the High Court justices with a legal, moral, and intellectual challenge. The essence of this challenge is a request that the justices examine the extent to which the plan was guided by the principle of equality. Attorney Feldman mentions at the beginning of the petition that, "...the sovereignty of the State of Israel has not been applied to the area of Ma`aleh Adumim, and its administration is based on international law, military orders, and Israeli laws that have seeped through..." He will claim that the expansion plan is meant to serve a population that lives within the boundaries of the State of Israel.

Basing his arguments on the expert opinions of two architects and urban planners—Professor Hubert Law-Yone of the Technion[3] and Shmuel Groag of Jerusalem—Feldman will demonstrate that the Ma`aleh Adumim expansion plan is compatible with the Jerusalem Metropolis Plan prepared in 1994 by a number of government ministries. The latter plan, whose purpose is "to establish and strengthen Jerusalem's status as the 'eternal' capital of Israel," assimilates the expanded city of Ma`aleh Adumim into "Greater Jerusalem." The plan forecasts a 285% increase in Ma`aleh Adumim's population between 1994–2010. For the Palestinian population, the Jerusalem Metropolis Plan forecasts a natural growth of only 17.1%. While the Jerusalem Metropolis Plan has not been granted legal status, according to the petitioners, "it was the 'spirit' behind the plan to expand Ma`aleh Adumim."

Almost 25 years after the establishment of Ma`aleh Adumim, Feldman will remind the justices that according to international law Israel and the territories are not subject to the same laws, and that an occupied territory must not be subjugated to the economic, political, social, and demographic interests of the occupying nation. International law restricts the powers of a military occupation, states the petition, "because it controls a politically helpless population… devoid of legal means to resist the power of the military occupier or even to take part in the decision-making process that governs its fate. The disadvantage and powerlessness of the occupied population are compensated for by international law—agreed upon by the community of civilized nations— which obliges them to keep their own power in check."

A considerable portion of the petition is devoted to the discrimination Ma`aleh Adumim's expansion would cause the Palestinian civilian population. "Within the disputed area, two communities conduct their lives. One has political power and the other is completely deprived of all democratic rights enjoyed by the residents of an enlightened country... The respondents failed to fulfill their administrative responsibility to attend equally to the needs of all the national groups living in the area." By means of military injunctions, the petition states, the settlements created islands of democracy for Jews alone. "This extensive legislation has created a situation unprecedented in the democratic world, in which two nationalities live in one territorial unit, one endowed with the rights of an enlightened democratic state based on the principles of justice, freedom, and equality, and the other controlled by a military government which is not democratic and is not subject to these principles. One has significant influence, as does the public in a democratic state," and the other is denied the right to representation.

In the petitioners' opinion, the Supreme Planning Council, by taking away "the land reserves from the petitioners' villages, created a situation wherein the Palestinian residents live in conditions of overcrowding 25 times greater than those in Ma`aleh Adumim... any objective criterion would have required that a similar amount of land and planning resources be allocated to the Palestinian villages."

The B'Tselem report also elaborates on the discrimination embodied in the very construction of Ma`aleh Adumim (and the settlements generally). But Captain Lerner, the Civil Administration spokesman, refutes this claim as well: "Ma`aleh Adumim was established on unsettled land... No houses or residents were removed for the purpose of [its] establishment... The area of Ma`aleh Adumim is desert land unsuitable for agriculture, which certainly cannot provide a family with livelihood... The establishment of Ma`aleh Adumim and the industrial zone Mishor Adumim created hundreds of jobs for the Palestinian residents of the area."

Lerner also mentions the land reserves available to the villages west of Ma`aleh Adumim: `Anata has 377 dunams;

`Azariya and Abu Dis together have 3,894 dunams. This land, writes Lerner, "provides for territorial contiguity in Area B, which can be developed by the Palestinian Authority without any restrictions from the Israeli side." Furthermore, adds Lerner, there are 12,000 dunams in Area C that are not state lands, which can also be used.

In his response, Lerner reflects the common Israeli view that state lands are off limits to Palestinians. The latter are permitted to develop on an individual basis in accordance with the amount of land they were lucky enough register as private. But they cannot do so as a community, over the entire geographic area in which they live. Using sophisticated legal methods, Israel has, since 1967, continuously expanded its definition of state lands. Before 1967, 527,000 dunams of the West Bank[4] were registered as state lands by the Jordanian government. By 1993, another 2 million dunams were added to this category. Even after the Oslo Accords were signed, these lands are still designated for the exclusive use of the Jewish population—a population belonging to a state whose internationally recognized borders do not include these lands.

———

1. The Israeli Information Center for Human Rights in the Occupied Territories.

2. 1 dunam = 1/4 acre.

3. The Israel Institute of Technology.

4. 5.5 million dunams in total.

PART TWO

(2000)

"The peace of the brave, of course!"

March 13, 2000

Recently, a group of Palestinian academics, intellectuals, and artists disseminated an extraordinary communiqué addressed to the "Israeli and Jewish Public."[1] Signatory to it are about 120 men and women whose lives encapsulate 20th century Palestinian history: 1948 refugees, 1967 displaced persons, people who returned in 1995, and people who continue to live in the diaspora. There are those who experienced the years of Israeli occupation since 1967, and others who became acquainted with Israelis in preliminary, forbidden talks in European capitals. Among them are university researchers and professors, painters, writers, poets, and journalists. They promise that they represent a broad Palestinian consensus, when they write to Israelis on the eve of final status negotiations: "We are concerned that what is being contrived is not peace, but the seeds of future wars."

"The majority of Palestinians believed that peace would be based on two principles: justice and the requirements of a common future. What we are witnessing in reality is far from these principles. One side believes the present balance of power to be in its favor, and that it can impose a humiliating agreement on the other side, forcing it to accept virtually anything it chooses to enforce. The historic settlement is becoming a settlement between Israelis themselves, not a settlement with the Palestinians."

Poet Zakaria Muhammad is among the signatories. At a corner cafe in Ramallah, he formulates his sentences with care. "We have grown tired of the wars, tired of the revolutions, and the Intifadas, and the blood. But we do not believe that the peace taking shape now will put an end to the wars and the chaos. On the contrary, perhaps there will be peace with a small group, with the negotiators, with the Palestinian Authority (PA), under pressure from the nations of the world, the Arab states, and Israel." But it is laden with explosives.

To Muhammad, who is a senior editor of *al-Karmel*, the leading Palestinian literary journal, it is clear that "what is taking shape now will end in some form of apartheid: a people that rule over another people, and a state that rules over another entity, which is not a state. The Palestinians will live in isolated bits and pieces of the country, which will increase their frustration and despair." Muhammad, who, since 1967 has lived in Jordan, Lebanon, Syria, and Iraq, says that "many people in the Arab world believe that what is taking shape is Arab submission to Israel and the Americans; that this is a humiliating arrangement" that will push various forces to war against Israel. "Therefore, we said to ourselves, for the sake of peace and coexistence, it is important that we address the Israeli public, Israeli intellectuals, and tell them that what is developing is not peace with the Palestinian people."

The communiqué deconstructs the emerging compromise "between the Israelis [and] themselves... a settlement that is imposed by a balance of forces overwhelmingly favoring your government and your military..." It is "a settlement," they write, "that suffocates the Palestinians humanly, territorially, security-wise, and politically: humanly, because it does not recognize their human and historical rights; territorially, because it isolates them within confined areas in towns and villages while progressively confiscating their land; security-wise because it places Israeli security in principle over and above Palestinian rights, existence and security; politically, because it prevents Palestinians from determining their future and controlling their borders."

Jamil Hilal is a sociologist. The 1967 war caught him studying in London. He was permitted to return after the signing of the Oslo Accords, and he works as a researcher at Bir Zeit University and the Palestine Economic Policy Research Institute (MAS) in Ramallah. Hilal was one of the initiators and formulators of the communiqué, but even before he enters the café, he tries, though not very successfully, to come across as full of sound and fury about how they "are hassling me like this on a Friday morning." That's Jamil, say his friends with a forgiving smile, never happy.

It is his colleague Zakaria Muhammad, the poet, who first addresses the sociopolitical context of the communiqué. Over the past three or four years, the Palestinian political arena has been paralyzed. The traditional political organizations, the ones associated with the PLO, did not know how to deal with the gap between the aspiration for independence and the enormous frustration generated by ongoing Israeli control over Palestinian life, and the PA's mode of governance. People turned inward to their personal lives and despaired of the public arena. But in recent months, a new trend has been developing. People are looking, once again, for a way to reorganize democratic political thinking, outside the political parties, which no longer offer relevant modes of action. Drafting a communiqué with political and social principles, which reflect the opinions of many, has brought a lot of supporters together.

Until now, manifestoes have been directed at Palestinian audiences or the PA. Now comes a communiqué directed at Israelis. Among the signatories are Dr. Haidar Abdel Shafi and members of the legislative council like Hanan Ashrawi and Kamal al-Sharafi (a doctor from Jabalya). Jamal Zakkout, a leading Intifada[2] activist who has been part of the Palestinian negotiating team since 1994, also signed it. It is signed by Palestinian feminist scholars Eileen Kuttab, Islah Jad, and Rima Hammami; artists Kamal Boullata, Taysir Barakat, and Khaled Hourani; and economists Samir Abdallah and Hisham Sharabi.

They, and their colleagues, write to the Israelis that they "see only two solutions for a just settlement of the Palestine question. The first solution is based on the establishment of a Palestinian state, with complete sovereignty over the lands occupied by Israel in 1967 and Jerusalem as its capital, the right of return for Palestinian refugees, and the recognition by Israel of the historic injustice inflicted on the Palestinian people. The Palestinian state will be established on the principles of democracy and human values adopted by the Palestinian Declaration of Independence in 1988. The second solution is the establishment of a democratic bi-national state for the two peoples on the historic land of Palestine."

Hilal explains the timing of the communiqué: "The beginning of the talks on the final status agreement. And this is a message to both the Israeli and the Palestinian negotiators: if you are going to make peace, peace has its own conditions. I do not expect that in September, or any other date in the near future, an agreement will be signed that will answer the requirements of a just peace. I do not believe that Barak will suddenly see the light. And I hope," says Hilal, choosing his words carefully, "that Arafat will not sign a humiliating agreement. I do not think that any leader could sign such a thing, and survive."

As to why the 1967 borders are the realistic ones, while many Jewish Israelis, including members of the peace camp, claim that a return to them is impossible, Hilal says: "Here it is possible to find a broad consensus among the Palestinians. Here the facts come into play: the vast majority of the population that lives within the 1967 borders is Palestinian, there is continuity from the period before 1948, and there are international resolutions that recognize this border." However, it is true that continued Israeli construction in the territories is bringing about a situation in which "the only possible solution will be a democratic bi-national state. If we are thinking of a stable future," he adds. "If Israelis think that up until now the politics of supremacy have indeed paid off," says Hilal, "they should remember 1973.

After the shock and humiliation [of 1967], the Arabs could do nothing but attack."

Among the Palestinians, too, notes Muhammad, "there are those who are saying: don't come to any agreement with the Israelis, because in 20 years things will change, and when we fight them, we will defeat them. 'The future is ours, not theirs,' they say." Precisely because the signatories to the communiqué agree with the assessment that "in 20 years everything could turn around and reverse itself," in a region where 200-250 million Arabs live, they are convinced that an agreement must not have humiliating elements that will undermine it in advance. Muhammad: "The reliance on force shows shortsightedness. We do not want to go back to the period of 1973, when there was a question mark floating over Israel, and it found that the atomic bomb was its only refuge."

"It is clear," they warn in the communiqué, "that the Palestinian negotiator, whose hands are tied by the overwhelming balance of power working against him, may be coerced into accepting a humiliating and degrading settlement... We want to tell [you] that the settlement the Israeli leadership is seeking to impose on the Palestinian negotiator [will] not be a settlement with the Palestinian people. It will be a fragile settlement bearing within it the seeds of its own destruction. We will neither support nor accept it."

Both Muhammad and Hilal "feel at home in Haifa, Acre, and Jaffa," just as they do in Nablus and Ramallah. But they do not derive their political solution from this. Personally, they would prefer to live in a bi-national state. But such a solution cannot be born of coercion. "No one can stop me from feeling that Jaffa is Palestine. Just as a Jew will feel that Nablus is part of the Land of Israel," says Muhammad. "You call it Israel, and I call it Palestine, and it is one land."

Both of them mention that in "this little country" any Jew

from the United States or Russia has the right to settle and become a citizen, but not the refugee from Shatila camp in Lebanon. In Muhammad's opinion, "after the Palestinian right of return is recognized, the best way to implement it will be found. This is not a matter of two or three months, but first of all, there must be Israeli recognition of the injustice perpetrated in 1948." Hilal adds, "The Israelis must say: 'Yes, you as Palestinians fell victim to a great injustice. Let us sit down and see what can be mended.'"

The vehement opposition to including Mahmoud Darwish's poems in the Israeli literary curriculum worries them both. In Hilal's opinion, "it is proof, albeit symbolic, that the Israeli public is not prepared to make peace with us." And Muhammad puts a finer point on this observation: "The sense is that the Israelis want to make peace with Arafat, but not with Mahmoud Darwish and Edward Said. But why? Peace will ultimately be signed with them," the representatives of the people's deep feelings.

Nonetheless, the signatories to the communiqué are trying to reach the Israeli public, which for the past six years has seen meetings with Arafat and senior members of his security apparatus as the face of peace. It is our obligation, they say, to speak out. The onus is on Israelis in general, and Israeli intellectuals in particular, to respond and take responsibility. "We extend our hand to you to make a real and just peace, not the militarist peace of coercion, the generals' peace."

---

1. Quotes from the communiqué are taken verbatim from the English translation circulated by the signatories.

2. The first Intifada of 1987–1992.

April 30, 2000

A small bunch of mint from the village of Dura al-Qara` will cost you one shekel at the Ramallah market. Mint from other places is much cheaper: four bunches for a shekel. The same is true for eggplant, squash, tomatoes, green beans, and spinach; people will pay four times what they would for vegetables from anywhere other than Dura—renowned for its fine produce.

The secret behind the superior taste and quality: Dura's farmers use only natural spring water to irrigate their small plots. The mere mention of chemical pesticides or tap water—let alone purified sewage—elicits a look of disgust on these farmers' faces. Nor does car exhaust reach this fertile valley—altogether 40 dunams[1] of cultivated land supporting 142 families—for a mountainside shelters it from the old Ramallah-Nablus highway.

The Palestinian Ministry of Tourism designated the valley a nature reserve, with the intention of turning it into a site where people can observe the traditional agricultural way of life. True, Dura al-Qara` is still in Area C, meaning under Israeli civil and security control. But Palestinian officials told themselves, and their people, that this is but a temporary administrative division of the West Bank, and that after negotiations over the interim agreement, they will gain control not only of the crowded urban centers, but the surrounding cultivated and undeveloped lands as well.

The valley of Dura al-Qara`—a five minute ride from the bustle of Ramallah and al-Bireh, which seem to be filling up with more cars, supermarkets, pizzerias, and housing projects every day—is steeped in an ancient tranquility and the harmony of man and nature. Seven springs flow forth from the western hillside. Abu Muhammad Hamdan, 50, who has spent most of his life working this land, names one of them: "'Ayn Mghara" (Cave Spring). "Believe me, in the winter the water is warm, and in the summer cold as if it came out of the fridge." He leads us to another spring, where lactating mothers are sent. They drink the water and "believe me, their breasts fill with milk." The spring is called "'Ayn al-Dar"—*dar* meaning milk but also abundance.

The spring water, less abundant than in years past, is channeled into a network of canals, small dams, and little reservoirs, which the villagers built decades ago. Thus, the water reaches every parcel. And each parcel, a few square meters in all, is subdivided into smaller, equidistant sections.

Thanks to the canals, the farmers maintain a water distribution system devised before their grandfathers were born: each family is allocated water in relation to the size of their plot. Recently, they began running black plastic hoses along the canals to save water and keep it clean. Water samples are taken and examined in a laboratory at Bir Zeit University every few months. "We are afraid," explains Abu Muhammad, "that the sewage from Beit El[2] will seep into the ground and contaminate our water."

On the slopes surrounding the valley, on terraces that no one can recall when or by whom they were built, ancient fruit trees grow: olive, mulberry, pear, almond, pomegranate, lemon. These are surrounded by wild herbs and bushes that the villagers use: sumac, nettle, mallow, chicory, mustard, and wild mint—whose pungent scent mixes with that of the milder, cultivated mint grown by two elderly farmers, each in his own plot. Red poppies dot the hills, and the only audible sounds in the spring air are those of birds, children who have dared check the water temperature in one of the reservoirs, and words exchanged between Palestinian Ministry of Agriculture workers who have come to reinforce a terrace wall.

The valley is also a favorite spot for soldiers and settlers; they can be seen hiking through, armed with guns and maps, bending down to taste the water. Some have left their handiwork behind: "The Nation of Israel Lives!" (dated March 2000) and here, a slightly faded bit of graffiti on the reservoir wall: "Death to the Arabs!"

If the plans of the Ministry of Defense, the Unit for Settlement and National Infrastructure, the Civil Administration's Supreme Planning Council for Judea and Samaria, and the Subcommittee for Roads and Railroads are realized, this valley will be destroyed in a few months' time. These Israeli institutions have decided— in the middle of final status negotiations—to pave a road connecting Ofra[3] and Beit El to shorten the distance between these two settlements defined as "isolated."[4]

It is difficult to call this road a "bypass road": it will cut through the cultivated lands of four Palestinian villages, and one of its forks will run straight into the Jalazoun Refugee Camp, alongside the UNRWA[5] school, necessitating the demolition of several houses both inside and outside the camp. The Knesset Committee for the Security Budget approved the plan for this road on April 10th, together with plans for another two-dozen bypass roads throughout the West Bank. Some ten roads are currently under construction, and in need of completion funding. All together, they will cost over 114 million NIS. The Ofra-Beit El road (36 million NIS) is on a list of roads not yet begun, which will cost a total of 510 million NIS.

The Civil Administration, which completed the plan in January 2000, published a standard notice in the Palestinian press on March 22nd. Using a dry bureaucratic tone, posing as fair, it posted "detailed master plan 924/3 for road number 4491 'Jalazoun-Ayn Yabroud' (which will connect road number 605 to road number 60)." The plan, it said, was submitted by the Department of Public Works and prepared by the Civil Engineering and Survey Company, Inc.

Contrary to the plan presented to the government for approval, the announcement in the Palestinian press does not mention the names Ofra and Beit El. The Arabic notice details all the parcels through which the road will pass: al-Bireh, Jifna (on whose lands the Jalazoun Refugee Camp is located), Dura al-Qara' (which will suffer the most damage), Silwad, and Ayn Yabroud. The notice invites members the public who feel they will suffer damages as a result of the expropriation to submit their objections within two months of the notice's date of publication—May 22, 2000.

Adding insult to injury is the very name "Civil Administration." Since its establishment in the early 1980s, it has disguised itself as an institution that sees to the needs of the "locals," hence the pretense of posting a notice in Arabic as if the road was intended to serve the Palestinian public. Not one of the villages mentioned needs it, nor do the residents of Ramallah and al-Bireh. A paved road already connects Ramallah and the villages of Beitin and Ayn Yabroud, from which one simply continues northward to the other villages. An unpaved road also connects Ayn Yabroud and Dura al-Qara'. The Ofra-Beit El road, however, will decapitate hilltops and pass 5 meters above the cultivated valley. It will be 5.9 kilometers long, 25 meters wide, and usurp 370 dunams. Alongside the road, 80 meters in each direction, "any construction which is not integral to the road" will be prohibited, including "water pipes, cables, gutters, canals, or any other means of provision or refuse... without first obtaining permission from the Supreme Planning Council." Not only is it forbidden to build alongside roads that serve settlements, experience shows that Palestinian landowners are also denied access to their nearby fields and orchards, which then wither due to forced neglect. And even if access is not denied, the negative impact of dirt, noise, asphalt, bridges, ramps, fences, and walls is easy to foresee.

The insult-to-injury factor only increases when it comes to Jalazoun, on whose margins a clearing is planned to make room for the new road. Dozens of refugees will be forced to leave their homes once again and stand by as they are demolished for the sake of Jewish development. Many Jalazoun residents are refugees from Beit Naballah (east of Lydda), which in the year 1596 had 297 residents, and in 1945 had 2,310. Abu Suleiman remembers the exodus from his village in 1948: "The Israeli army surrounded the village, a plane bombarded us from the air, and we fled." In his book, *The Birth of the Palestinian Refugee Problem: 1947–1949*, historian Benny Morris mentions Beit Naballah as one of the villages evacuated upon orders from the Arab Legion. Palestinian historian Walid Khalidi, however, has found no evidence to substantiate this claim.

Upon resettling in Jalazoun, Abu Suleiman and his sons engaged in petty commerce. They saved their pennies with determination and one purpose in mind: to get out of the center of the camp, buy a little land on its margins, build a more spacious home, and return to farming. The small dairy built by one of his sons last year is now slated for demolition. "Every clod of earth," says another son, who just returned from studying in the US, "we bought with the sweat of our labors." "Where shall we go now?" asks Um Suleiman, and her husband echoes the same question. Where will they find the money to buy an alternate plot, now that prices have skyrocketed; land purchased 20 years ago for thousands of dollars cannot be touched today for tens of thousands. They wonder about the logic guiding Israeli planners: they built the Ramallah bypass road so the settlers could avoid the stones thrown from Jalazoun. Now they are paving a road that hundreds of refugee children will cross daily on their way to and from school. So they are bringing the settlers back to the stones that everyone knows will be thrown—for what other weapon do the dispossessed have?

Everyone—young and old, opposition forces and PA security personnel—is asking the same questions and awaiting the inevitable confrontation. Faeq Hamdan, 41, a senior Fatah activist who spent nine years in Israeli prisons, and serves as an officer in one of the Palestinian Authority (PA) security services, foresees that the destruction of the valley "will impoverish the people. It will obliterate a traditional way of life that people like, and from which they make an honorable living. Moreover, not only will it destroy the loveliest bit of nature in the Ramallah area, it will help to isolate Ramallah from the other cantons."

As a Fatah man, he attests that he has spent the last few years "educating the youth to believe in peaceful coexistence with Israel. And here, one Israeli road comes along and wipes out all my efforts. What Israel teaches them with this road, is that it is interested in one thing—violence."

---

1. 1 dunam = 1/4 acre.

2. Israeli settlement northeast of Ramallah, population: 4,000.

3. Israeli settlement northeast of Ramallah, population: 2,000.

4. Settlements not part of a contiguous "bloc."

5. United Nations Relief Works Agency.

May 3, 2000

How very accurate is the Hebrew word that defines a strip of asphalt as *kvish*. How precise Modern Hebrew was when it created this definition from the three-letter root *Kaf-Bet-Shin*. How perfectly this common word, when it enters the realm of Israeli-Palestinian relations, takes on the harsh dimensions of this root, which is also the root of the Hebrew word for occupation or conquest—*kibbush*—meaning: to subordinate, to oppress, to crush, to defeat.

The main road that links the (annexed) neighborhoods of north Jerusalem with al-Bireh[1] and Ramallah is under Israeli sovereignty.

Because here we talk about a "united Jerusalem, the eternal capital of Israel," at least for now the road itself is an integral part of these verbal fireworks. This main artery is used by tens of thousands of Palestinians every day, as well as by IDF and Border Police vehicles.

Numerous winding bypass roads have been built for Jewish Israeli citizens in recent years. These roads are longer, but travel on them is faster, of shorter duration, and most importantly, safer. They are spacious, smoothly paved, and equipped with lane separators and traffic lights. Compared with them, travel on the "Palestinian" road is a perilous obstacle course. There are potholes, patches, broken traffic lights, broken or nonexistent sidewalks, and faded or nonexistent signposts. It is easy to see at what point on the road Israeli jurisdiction ends and Palestinian civil control begins: at the entrance to al-Bireh, where over a year ago the continuation of the road was upgraded. There, the wheels straighten out again and stop swerving as if they were drunk.

The police have been warning the Jerusalem municipality that this is a "red artery" and that without adequate sign-posting, it is almost impossible to enforce traffic regulations. The municipality agrees that sometimes it is "life-threatening," applies a patch or two, and continues to regard the appalling road under its jurisdiction as if it were a natural phenomenon beyond its control, and not a case of decades of systematic neglect (on the part of the municipality itself); a road whose only sin is that it serves Palestinians. And thus the word for road, and its root, take on another meaning: fatal discrimination.

Along comes a Japanese donation of about $6 million for the United Nations Development Program (UNDP) to refurbish the road and carry out the work. But at the municipality, they are sticking to the law. It is illegal for the Palestinian Authority (PA) to operate within Israeli territory, the donation is part of Japan's contributions to the PA, and the UNDP is only mandated to operate within PA territory. As the municipality sees it, allowing the UNDP to improve the road is like, heaven help us, relinquishing the perpetuity of its sovereignty in Jerusalem. At the municipality they would, of course, not object to the Japanese rerouting the donation and transferring the funds to Israel and its Jewish contractors instead of the UNDP and its Palestinian contractors. Thus, to the root *Kaf-Bet-Shin* another meaning is added: *chutzpa*.[2]

The money that Israel has not found to upgrade the road between Jerusalem and Ramallah, it has found and will continue to find for the construction of some two dozen "bypass" roads in the West Bank, approved at the beginning of April. In the Israeli registry one of these roads is called "Ofra-Beit El" and will serve the Jewish inhabitants of these settlements. In official notices published by the Civil Administration in the Palestinian press it is called the "Jalazoun-Ayn Yabroud" road. This road, if it comes into being (like its predecessors), will damage hundreds of dunams of cultivated Palestinian land, devastate a beautiful landscape, and destroy once and for all an agricultural way of life preserved at will by the inhabitant of the village of Dura al-Qara`. The road, approved by the Labor-Meretz-Shas-NRP[3] government, will also demolish several homes in the Jalazoun Refugee Camp. The magic phrase "bypass road" is enough to make everyone stand at attention when it comes to "the security of Jewish inhabitants." And thus, the word for road, and its root, take on yet another meaning: deceit.

The plan for this destructive road (36 million NIS—more than it would cost to improve the Jerusalem-Ramallah road) does not fool the Palestinians. They are convinced that it is not meant to meet transportation needs, but Israel's strategic aims to dictate the terms of the final status agreement once negotiations commence. Will the Palestinians be able to tolerate the paving of another 24 occupation-perpetuating roads? To the meanings of the word for road in Hebrew a note of warning has been added: time bomb.

---

1. Palestinian town southeast of Ramallah, population: 30,000.

2. Hebrew for nerve / audacity.

3. National Religious Party.

May 28, 2000

Where the persuasive efforts of Palestinian political organizations, the pleas of the heads of the Palestinian educational system, the resignation of the director-general of the Education Ministry (not accepted), and threats, arrests, and venomous rumors failed, Nakba Day succeeded. On May 15th, the day that marks the Palestinian catastrophe, bloody confrontations between Palestinian demonstrators and the IDF left three Palestinians dead and hundreds wounded. After the carnage, the Supreme Coordinating Committee of Palestinian teachers in state schools decided, in an urgent telephone conference, to stop the battle it has been waging since February. The general strike that the 17,935 teachers at all 1,069 government schools in the West Bank planned to hold on May 16th was canceled, and all 412,190 students returned to school as scheduled.

This strike is like any other: workers compete for favorable public opinion against treasury officials and cabinet ministers. The workers demand raises, which they feel are mandated by the importance of their profession and the welfare of the younger generation; the authorities admit that while the situation is not easy, there are constant improvements and wage increases. The former point out that in the first year of work a married teacher with no children earns a basic monthly salary of 943 NIS, which travel reimbursements and supplements bring to 1,451 NIS; the latter spell out all the benefits that teachers receive. The former ask how, at level 3 on the salary scale and with 23 years' seniority, a married teacher can support his five children on a basic salary of 1,415 NIS, which after travel reimbursements and supplements reaches 2,045 NIS; the latter agree that it is hard, but the national situation requires unity and sacrifice.

But this battle, which the teachers have been waging for three years, and which everyone expects will continue into the coming school year, is another chapter in the book Palestinian society is writing on the struggle for independence and democracy. This is not a chapter being written by university professors taking part in one-day conferences on "civil society and the problems of democratization." We are talking about thousands of teachers, many of whom, according to Omar Assaf, have to supplement their income after school by driving taxis, pumping gas, serving food in restaurants and cafes, or sweating over bakery ovens.

Assaf, 50, is one of the three spokespersons appointed by the Supreme Coordinating Committee of the striking teachers. The exact number of committee members (drawn from local teachers' committees in every district) and their identities remain ambiguous for security reasons. Three years ago, in the Spring of 1997, when the teachers launched the battle for wage increases, the Palestinian Authority (PA) responded with a wave of arrests, starting with members of the coordinating committee. It is difficult, of course, to hide the activists' identities from the Palestinian security apparatus. According to testimony gathered by Qanun (LAW), the Palestinian Society for the Protection of Human Rights and the Environment, many teachers have been called in for questioning in recent months, queried about their political orientation, and asked to sever their ties with the local coordinating committees and desist from protest activities. They were also warned of the implications that refusal to meet their interrogators' demands could have. These pressure tactics have worked over time, says one of the organizers, particularly on the younger, more inexperienced activists, and especially on those associated with the Islamic movements. It is always easier to arrest them and to boast that the issue at hand is the war against terror.

Pressure tactics also worked on activists associated with Fatah, many of whom announced their resignation from the committees.

But new members are voted in all the time, while the core group of activists remains the same: teachers who gained experience as leaders of an "illegal" trade union under Israeli occupation.

For the past three years the teachers have been demanding, in addition to wage increases, that general elections be held for a union that would represent all teachers in state schools. Officially, such a union exists: The General Union of Palestinian Teachers (GUPT), which is supposed to represent all teachers in the occupied territories and the diaspora. It was founded in 1992, when the Israeli occupation authorities withdrew their opposition to its establishment. But its members were appointed from above and, not surprisingly, most were associated with the Fatah. On July 6, 1997, a petition signed by 10,000 teachers was submitted to the PA asking to be represented by a union that is elected, rather than appointed. In response, the union's leadership was reappointed in October 1999, and 15 of its 22 members were, again, from the Fatah. Not surprisingly, the appointed leaders announced that the teachers' demands were justified, but that their struggle should not be waged through strikes in this time of "national emergency." And what a coincidence—a number of GUPT appointees hold senior positions in PA ministries.

Assaf and the rest of the teachers are tired of the national struggle being exploited as a means to silence their activism. "Our situation here, our situation as a nation—is always difficult, and we face hardships continuously, so it is impossible to keep on saying that we must take the situation into consideration and wait for a more appropriate time," he stresses. One of his fellow strikers says that these days the national struggle and the class struggle complement each other; they should not be separated because the struggle against occupation and for independence requires a strong society that feels that its leadership respects it and sees to the welfare of all its members.

Assaf had a golden opportunity to explain the reasons for the strike in a live broadcast on Love and Peace, a local Ramallah radio station. The program was aired on Wednesday, May 3rd. Early on the morning of May 5th, some 20 policemen knocked on his door, "You will find him at the Ramallah police station," they told his wife. Assaf is still in detention.

According to attorneys from Qanun, the president of the Ramallah district court reviewed the case and decided that the arrest was illegal. But as usual, no one in the Palestinian executive branch listens to decisions by the judiciary when it comes to arbitrary arrests.

And so, the striking teachers are demanding that, first of all, the executive branch honor the laws passed by the Palestinian legislature; in other words, the principles of the rule of law and the separation of powers. Their salary demands are grounded in the Public Sector Law, which finally passed in October 1998 after endless deliberations (and exhaustive lobbying with PA Chairman Yasser Arafat). The law mandates a large and immediate salary increase to most public sector workers, particularly in health and education. But the law's implementation has been frozen since it was passed, and in the meantime teachers' wages have eroded by some 22%. In the interview that led to his arrest, Assaf reiterated that, "All we are asking for is the implementation of the law passed by the Palestinian Legislative Council and signed by the Chairman."

Implementing the Public Sector Law over the past two years would have cost $100 million. Addressing claims by Palestinian treasury officials that there is no money in the budget for the increase, Assaf reminded his listeners of what they already knew: the four commercial monopolies that the PA continues to operate (despite repeated promises to the donor countries that they would be disbanded) hold the exclusive right to import and market flour, tobacco, concrete, and fuel. Profits from these companies, Assaf explained on the air, are not transferred into the open funds of the Ministry of Finance from which the annual budget is composed, but rather into hidden funds. The profits total $400 million a year. "What do you mean $400 million, it's at least $800 million," interjected one of his colleagues from the Democratic Front for the Liberation of Palestine (DFLP), but there is no way of knowing the exact amount.

Particularly prominent among the leaders of the strike are members of the DFLP and the People's Party (formerly the Communist Party), two relatively small organizations in the Palestinian political arena. One of the teachers evades the obvious question, "Why you?" It's the ideology, the party backing and, of course, the long years of struggle against Israeli occupation. Assaf, who is a member of the DFLP's political bureau, has been imprisoned in Israeli jails, and during the Intifada[1] was wanted for his activism and spent some time underground.

The evasive teacher explains: "It's not that I hide my political affiliation from the PA, that is exactly what the PA is trying to claim: that political affiliation is what drives us, that we are motivated by resistance to the PA (and the Oslo process), and not by our class consciousness. That is exactly how it was under Israel: when we demanded a trade union, we were told it was a cover organization for the PLO. And I know that tomorrow they will say that we are collaborators for talking to an Israeli journalist."

In the radio interview, Assaf complained about the secondary importance afforded to education in the Palestinian budget. In three years, he said, the proportion of the budget devoted to education dropped from 22% to about 16%. A report by the Palestinian legislature at the beginning of the year names a higher figure of 18%, but notes with concern the same downward trend: $166 million for education, compared to $400 million for security.

The radio station that broadcast Assaf's interview was closed for a few days by the PA, like the al-Nauras television station in Hebron, which broadcast an interview with striking teachers back in February. The strike, which ended last week, began last February as a local issue in Bethlehem—in protest of the introduction of a new pension law that requires every civil servant to make retroactive pension payments from the time he or she began working, at rates ranging from 2%-10% of their current salary. The strike spread to Hebron (which has the largest number of schools and teachers) and then to Ramallah. Gradually, it crept northward, and the coordinating committee reconvened, issuing weekly announcements to organize the modes of protest, times of demonstrations, and strike days. The implementation of the pension law was frozen, but PA officials refused to meet with representatives of what they consider to be an illegal and non-representative organization.

The Legislative Council justified the teachers' demands, and pushed for the establishment of a joint ministerial and legislative commission in early April that promised to submit its recommendations for a decisive solution; that is, the implementation of the Public Sector Law, by May 1st. It also agreed to meet with members of the Supreme Coordinating Committee as representatives of the strikers, not the teachers. On April 8th the teachers agreed to suspend their protests until May 1st. In late April, it was rumored that there could be delays in the commission's decision-making process.

The pattern is a familiar one: the Palestinian leadership sets up a commission to discuss some public grievance; this generates a great deal of hoopla, and promises to solve the problem are scattered liberally, while the commission then fades into oblivion. The teachers' representatives were unwilling to cooperate with the well-known process of burying important issues. They warned that strikes would be renewed after May 1st, and indeed, when the commission's recommendations failed to arrive, they renewed the strike and began demonstrating on May 2nd. PA officials were furious, seeing this as sabotage of an understanding, since the commission's recommendations were supposed to be submitted to the Cabinet by May 5th. On May 5th the Cabinet did not discuss the recommendations, but Assaf was arrested. Immediately following his arrest a few demonstrations were held in Ramallah: first by the DFLP, then by teachers in the region, and finally, by the Refugees Association of Beit Naballah—Assaf's village of origin. Assaf, it is said, once taught Suha Tawil, also known as Suha Arafat.

---

1. The first Intifada of 1987–1992.

September 20, 2000

The conduct of Israeli negotiators is based, among other things, on the assumption that it is the Palestinians who will lose by rejecting an agreement, and that therefore, they must accept whatever is offered them now. In other words, Israel can afford to live, and live well, without an agreement.

This assumption is supported by a secondary assumption, propagated by elements in the Israeli security establishment, that even the Palestinians' most obvious bargaining chip—confrontation—is not feasible due to their economic dependence on Israel. It is worth noting that first, contrary to recent statements made by security elements, the policy of closure has not been "stopped completely" since 1997. Restrictions on Palestinians' freedom of movement are firm and abiding. Second, it is true that corruption in the Palestinian Authority (PA) is driving away investors, but so is political uncertainty and never-ending closure.

The two assumptions warrant examination, beginning with the secondary assumption. On the eve of the Intifada,[1] the Israeli security rationale was similar. The economic status of tens of thousands of Palestinian families had improved after 1967, when the Palestinians became Israel's cheap labor force and a few new refugee neighborhoods were built. In the words of an "offended" senior Israeli official in the office of the Coordinator of Government Activities in the Territories in 1992: "We built them Sheikh Radwan [a neighborhood in Gaza] and they still took part in the Intifada." Israel was blind to the non-economic factors that made life intolerable for every Palestinian. Nor did it understand that people compare their situation to the improved situation of their neighbors, especially when the latter have rights that the former are denied.

Another weak point of Israeli analysis is the focus on Arafat as the one responsible for instigating or reining in any potential confrontation. Rebellion is not planned from above, and the moment could come when the people who were not afraid of IDF rifles will not be put off by those wielded by the Palestinian police. Yet another blind spot is the disregard for the great poverty in which at least one-third of the Palestinian population lives. No intelligence officer can know when and how this poverty will give rise to opposition.

Israel under Prime Minister Ehud Barak has the unanimous support of the West. Should the Likud return to power, this could change. Will the military-economic elites in Israel withstand such a change?

Let's assume they will. How will Israel manage with the possible collapse of the PA as a result of the PLO's failure to justify its peace strategy? How will it manage with the mass yearning for Allah, and his earthly representatives—the Hamas movement? Look how much a similar Israeli response to years of oppression and discrimination—the Shas movement—threatens the existing order in Israel.

The Palestinians need not, or cannot, become Hizballah. But can Israel cope with even a limited version of this organization in the territories? Even if the PLO leadership remains in power, the Palestinian security forces will not agree to restrain Hamas indefinitely. How will Israel manage with the inevitable increase in the defense budget once the PA stops operating as a defense subcontractor? The Israelis—those who make the political and economic decisions—have grown accustomed to living well in recent years. The settlements and the "non-ideological" Jewish "neighborhoods" of East Jerusalem beckon to Israelis because of the quality of life they offer at a reasonable price. Will this Israeli middle class be able to adapt to constant harassment and the disruption of their comfortable lives—harassment whose scope or nature we can scarcely imagine today? How many lives will be sacrificed and how many years will pass before Israel's mothers ask why their sons must patrol the roads connecting Kfar Saba to the Jordan Valley?

The Palestinians are more accustomed than the Israelis to living poorly, and in uncertainty, and for longer periods of time. They have familial, social, and religious mechanisms that offer more protection in the face of economic and emotional hardships. By no means is it obvious that Israel, the military power, will win the contest between the two peoples over who can endure more suffering, and display a greater patience.

Meanwhile, a Palestinian assumption is also developing. If Israel does not understand that this may be its last chance to receive broad Palestinian consent to live in peace alongside a Jewish state within its 1967 borders, then the interim period can be stretched indefinitely, without determining borders, without even waging a struggle. Just let nature take its course. One day, there will be as many Palestinians in Israel (from the river to the sea) as there are Jews, at which point a different battle will be waged—like that in South Africa—"one person, one vote."

---

1. The first Intifada of 1987–1992.

October 10, 2000

At 9:30am on Monday, Love and Peace, a local Ramallah radio station, suddenly broadcast an advertisement. An ad? For three consecutive days, all the local radio and television stations played were sad songs or militant songs with a driving beat, opening their microphones to listeners grieving over the dead, wishing the injured well, and exalting the Prophet Muhammad. There were a few mishaps, such as yesterday morning, when a caller to the Voice of Palestine mentioned the detainees in Palestinian jails. The host interrupted him swiftly to say: "We do not have any detainees," please concentrate on what's happening today—the massacre, the struggle, the dead—thank you very much and good-bye. And the girl who read from a political leaflet: "We ask that our national authority not surrender and sign the deal the Americans want…" She too was cut off, politely, by the host, but not before being thanked for her contribution.

Every few minutes the programming was interrupted with updates on clashes and funerals: Tul Karm, Hebron, Beit Sahour, Idna.[1] And over and over again: Gaza, Rafah, Khan Yunis.[2] And then: Um al-Fahm, Nazareth, Jaffa.[3] The broadcasters continued to read out the names of the dead, the number of dead, and the location of death—ignoring the green line altogether.

That is why the advertisement was surprising. Was the state of emergency over? Had some secret agreement been reached? Since Sunday, when attempts to achieve calm began, Muhammad Dahlan, the head of Preventative Security in Gaza, repeated that it should not be called a "cease-fire." In his view, it was children facing one of the most powerful armies in the world. These are not two warring factions, he said. Israel must first withdraw its massive troops, lift the siege, and stop shooting to kill. The Palestinian television and radio stations are using the term "massacre."

Palestinian television shows the pictures of the wounded that Israeli television has spared its viewers. But Monday morning was strangely quiet around Ramallah. Many more Palestinian forces were deployed near IDF checkpoints; people say the same was true for Tul Karm and Khan Yunis. And there was a heightened presence of the elite Palestinian Force 17 around Yasser Arafat's headquarters. In the morning, they prevented cars from approaching the headquarters. Perhaps something happened overnight after all, and the advertisement was not accidental. But that was the only ad. So maybe it was a mistake after all.

The broadcasters announce the funeral times: 11:30 Palestine time, 12:30 Israel time—on Friday the clock was moved back to coincide with Jordan's. The clock is important when you work in Israel, but not when everything is closed and you are living in a hermetically sealed, isolated enclave. Then the hours, days, and months don't seem to matter.

In the midst of one of the clashes, someone who lives nearby extends an invitation for a cup of tea and recalls the Lebanese civil war: every day there was a two-hour lull in the fighting when people would hurry out to shop, visit friends, sit in a café—just to feel normal. Here, they run through the spray of machine guns fired by IDF soldiers, when minutes before they were sipping tea, or laughing at a joke. Someone runs head first into his own death, while another leans against a wall, nonchalantly warming himself in the autumn sun, watching the clashes from afar. No one gets angry with the onlookers; no one forces others to join in.

On Saturday, the Ministry of Education announced that the schools would strike in mourning: first a one-day strike was called, then it was extended until Tuesday. Yesterday, they announced that it would continue until next Saturday. It is the best way to guarantee that children do not head out to the army checkpoints en masse. When they are home, their parents can look after them, making sure that they stay in the yard. All the shops have been closed since Saturday, except for produce markets and grocery stores, which open their doors halfway, and an occasional carpentry workshop, gas station, or tire repair business. The mourning and uncertainty color everything: the calm broken by sirens and the incessant hum of Israeli helicopters, the black flags that are hung once again, the mother who shouts to her son not to stray too far on his scooter.

On Saturday morning thick smoke from burning tires obscures the soldiers at the Ayosh[4] junction, just to the south of the Civil Administration, the military court, and the settlement of Beit El. Palestinian policemen are stationed up the road, a few hundred meters from the site of the clashes. Among those watching is an old man in a white robe, a refugee who just arrived from Jordan, where he has lived since 1948. On Friday, before it all began, he visited the remains of his village, Bourj, near Beit Shemesh, for the first time since he fled it. He recognized every rock and tree, says his son in astonishment. The old man approaches a policeman and reprimands him: how can you stand by like that? The officer explains that his uniform does not negate his Palestinian-ness, and that he, from the Balata Refugee Camp, is thinking about his younger brother who must have gone out to throw stones at the soldiers near Joseph's Tomb, but he himself is a police officer in service of a government that has chosen a strategy of peace and so he does not use arms. If someone is killed, he says, he will shoot back.

He does not know that at that moment, a boy named Muhammad al-Dura is taking one bullet after another in his belly, dying in his wounded father's arms, at Netzarim Junction (the junction of the *Shuhada*—those who died in battle, in the Gaza Strip). Everything was captured on camera by Talal Abu

Rahme: who shouted at the soldiers to stop, who hid behind a van to avoid being shot himself, "and all I could do was to keep filming and crying."

That evening, and over the next two days, everyone spoke about the boy. The number of people at every intersection and checkpoint in the West Bank and Gaza doubled. The police officer from the day before was no longer willing to discuss the strategy of peace.

Near the Ayosh junction, a first-aid and triage station is set up, staffed by volunteers from the Union of Palestinian Medical Relief Committees, an NGO established 20 years ago by the Palestinian Communist Party. After the clashes of September 1996 (the "Tunnel Riots"), it was clear that the Palestinians knew how to run and get killed, but not how to provide first aid to the injured. And it was clear that there would be more clashes to come. The organization initiated a series of courses—attended by thousands—in evacuating the wounded, administering first aid, and managing states of emergency. No more carrying the wounded by hand; now there are bright green stretchers, and a doctor from the organization is also on hand. The staff decides whether a Ministry of Health ambulance should be called or if bandaging will suffice.

Saturday afternoon. At the al-Bireh junction hours go by as stones, burning tires, and Molotov cocktails are exchanged with rubber-coated bullets and live ammunition. Suddenly a mass of young people begins running in the opposite direction—that is, from the Israeli checkpoint back toward the city. "*Yahoud, yahoud*,"[5] they shout. "*Mist`arvim, mist`arvim*."[6] They are convinced that two photographers who crossed from the soldiers' side to that of the demonstrators, are Israeli soldiers disguised as Arabs. Proof—they do not speak or react in any language. Strange. The youths attack them, throwing stones and yelling. Someone rescues the two, puts them in a car, and tells them that Israelis are forbidden to enter. At some point shots are heard. Someone tries to drag them out of the car to lynch them. The Palestinian security forces shoot into the air in order to drive away the attackers. People say they were Fatah supporters from the al-'Amari Refugee Camp—whom everyone fears. Afterwards, it is said that it was their leader, a former political prisoner, who rescued the two photographers: a Russian and a Greek, by their names. One camera was taken, and waved in the air with hatred: a symbol of evil. Everyone is convinced that IDF snipers use television footage to track down the stone-throwers, and take them out. The incident worried some of the veteran activists.

On Monday the funeral procession of 'Imad al-'Anati sets out from al-'Amari camp. Al-'Anati was a member of Force 17, says the death notice. Twenty-nine years old. But someone from the camp says that he left the police and went back to the *Tanzim*,[7] to the Fatah. The procession heads for the al-Bireh cemetery. Everyone, like him, is from the Fatah. The forehead of the corpse, which is carried on a stretcher, is wrapped in a green band printed with verses from the Quran. Beneath his eye is a gaping, bleeding hole. There is one Palestinian flag, and a lot of green (Hamas) flags decorated with verses from the Quran being waved at this Fatah activist's funeral.

Directly above the cemetery, on a hill, is the settlement of Psagot. One of the elderly residents of the refugee camp relates that once, 20 years ago, he suggested to a landed family from al-Bireh that they set aside a few dozen dunams for some of the camp residents, to ease their overcrowding. The old man, in a derisive tone seething with anger, relates how the head of the family refused. A few years later the family's land was expropriated and the settlement of Psagot was built there instead. Now the family mourns the loss of its land.

After the funeral the camp residents set out, determined

and armed with stones, toward the settlement. Suddenly shots are fired at them from an unknown source, and they do not know where to take cover—that is the most frightening part. Someone dares to suggest that it was "Arabs" who shot at the camp residents—Palestinian policemen. The speaker is influenced by rumors of a pending agreement. "What's your problem," someone else says, "it wasn't Arabs it was Jews"—from the settlement. Screams: someone is wounded. Then: an ambulance siren. And the clashes and shooting go on for hours, until nightfall. That night there are reports of more clashes around Ramallah. It is difficult to decide what to do: run from one place to another or to watch television. In any event we won't reach Gaza today, even though the heart longs to be there, of all places. In gray Khan Yunis, across from green Neve Dekalim.[8] Now, say reports, houses in the western part of Khan Yunis are being evacuated for fear of an Israeli missile attack, or invasion.

But the television and radio stations bridge the distances, as does the Internet. On Sunday the prisoners' rights organization al-Damir launched a new website. It is updated every few hours, for users around the world, and those of us who wish they could be everywhere at once.

———

1. Palestinians communities in the West Bank.

2. Palestinian communities in the Gaza Strip.

3. Palestinian communities inside Israel.

4. Hebrew acronym for the Judea and Samaria region (West Bank).

5. Arabic for "Jews."

6. Hebrew for "undercover soldiers disguised as Arabs."

7. Arabic for "Organization." Common name for Fatah's armed wing during the second Intifada; denotes Fatah activists from within the occupied territories as opposed to those allowed to return from exile in the framework of the Oslo agreements to serve the PA.

8. Israeli settlement in the southern Gaza Strip, population: 2,500.

October 31, 2000

The only audible noise was that of an iron object knocking on cracked pavement. Then some footsteps. After that, a pause, two steps, iron knocking pavement, another pause, and some murmuring. Finally, two youths emerged, sweeping the deserted streets, and piling trash on a rickety wheelbarrow. They had big grins, and grimy faces and hands. After uttering some incoherent words it became clear that these were mentally handicapped children. The only people allowed out of the houses and into the streets of Hebron's Old City.

On Friday mornings, Hebron's market usually bustles with shoppers and merchants. But the 30,000-40,000 Palestinian residents of the Old City have been living under 24-hour curfew as prisoners in their own homes for over a month now. This is the part of Hebron classified as H2: from the market to the hilltop cemetery, including schools and alleys and sloping neighborhoods and the Ibrahimi Mosque (the Tomb of the Patriarchs). H2 is under Israeli control. Five hundred Jewish settlers live in Hebron's H2 section. The curfew does not apply to them.

We knocked on the iron door of one of the stone houses above the open market. Nobody answered. We tried another door, at an arched entrance nearby—nobody answered there either. But young voices could be heard emanating from a partially obscured stairwell. So we climbed the steep stairs, and knocked on the third door we came to.

Eleven members of the M family live in this rented, three-room apartment. There are nine children; six are school age and their first complaint is that they have not been allowed to study for a month. Their mother voices the same grievance. Thirty-four schools in Hebron have been shut down due to the curfew. Looking down from their rooftop, the family can see Jewish children being bussed to school (or anywhere else for that matter).

Meanwhile, these Palestinian kids walk back and forth idly in their small apartment, from the kitchen to the bedroom to the living room and back again. Late on the night of September 30th, an IDF jeep drove through the H2 streets, announcing in the hoarse metallic tones of a loudspeaker that residents were under curfew until further notice. Two streets away, in the H1 section—which is under Palestinian control—life goes on as usual: children go to school—providing these are not located in the H2 area. One house is under curfew, while from the neighboring house a young man emerges to go to mosque. Outside the H1 house, taxis drop off passengers at fresh produce stands, which are folded up along the walls in the afternoon, when clashes break out between Palestinian youth and IDF soldiers, resulting in the usual mix of stones, tear gas, burning tires, gunfire, explosions, and ambulance sirens.

During the first 15 days of the curfew, relates the mother of the M family, they could not leave the house at all. Twice during this two-week period strangers came and delivered basic foodstuffs. In the last two weeks, the curfew has been lifted five times, and in each instance, the hiatus lasted a few hours—a jeep circled the Old City streets announcing that the curfew would be suspended between this and that hour.

The simply furnished apartment is impeccably clean. One daughter sits on the floor next to an old washing machine laundering sheets. Only the mother and children are at home. The father, a construction worker who is out of work because of the curfew and who, his wife says, "hasn't brought home even 100 NIS this month," is not in the apartment. In the early dawn he darted across the rooftops, avoiding the soldiers' ubiquitous, peering eyes, to get away from the cramped, child-congested apartment.

"Even when the curfew is temporarily lifted," the mother says, "I'm afraid to send the children out. They announce that the pause will last a few hours, but, as happened a few days ago, some trouble arose on a nearby street; Molotov cocktails were thrown, and so they announced that the curfew was back in effect, and everyone had to return home. My children had wandered away, and I went out of my mind before I found them. And if they roam around the streets, what's going to happen if a settler sees them?"

"Our lives are death," she states flatly. "In the twenty years we've lived here, it has never been so bad. Not even after the massacre at the Ibrahimi Mosque." (The mass murder perpetrated by Baruch Goldstein on February 24, 1994). "There are no neighbors left around here. They have all fled—so it's empty and quiet. Just us. We have family outside, but we have not seen them for a month. They phone us—we have a mobile phone, but we can't use it to call out, because we don't have money for phone cards. Where am I supposed to get money for phone calls? There's only money for the most basic food items. The children understand the situation. They don't ask me to buy anything special, and they don't complain about the food."

The mother continues, "Our neighbors have all gone off to live with relatives. We're stuck in the house. The settlers roam the streets below. We hear them laughing and talking and carrying on, and we're imprisoned in the house. At night we hear shots—constant gunfire—and we sleep together in one room, in the back, as far as possible from the street below. We don't know what's going on or who is shooting; nor do we know how to call for help, should anything happen."

She adds, "A few days ago we heard an explosion, and then there was tear gas. The gas penetrated our apartment and choked us. My little children suffer from asthma, and they coughed and gagged and wept. I discovered that I didn't have enough medicine. I went out to get some, but a soldier wouldn't let me pass. I begged and explained that I needed to get some medicine, but he just yelled and told me to get back inside. In the end, I managed to call for a doctor to bring the medicine. Another time, I went out to get some bread, because we had run out, and a soldier stopped me at first, not wanting to let me through. But I was stubborn, and told him that I had children to feed, and in the end he let me pass. Our lives are death."

"This mosque," she says, pointing outside her window, "has been quiet for a month now. Not a single Muslim has come to pray here—neither here nor at the Ibrahimi Mosque. And we have not seen a single funeral at the cemetery across the way for a month. People are dying and can't be laid to rest there—where their ancestors are buried."

G's family has lived for decades in a house across from the cemetery on Shuhada Street—a Hebron thoroughfare used by Jewish settlers who come and go between the Beit Hadassah and Avraham Avinu neighborhoods. G's sisters and their children managed to leave the curfew-restricted home, and took up residence in the H1 section of the city. But G's mother insisted on staying in the house, and G and his brother, both bachelors, stayed on in the H2 domicile with her.

G's mother has lived in a house crammed with heavy wooden furniture, ceramic bric-a-brac, and lavish drapes and carpets for 45 years. When Baruch Goldstein perpetrated his massacre at the Ibrahimi Mosque, she found herself at the center of the gruesome scene. Since then, she has suffered from heart problems, and is due for a check-up at Jerusalem's al-Maqassed hospital, but cannot leave her Hebron home to get there. Her chest aches, and her left arm throbs, but aside from worrying, she has no idea what to do or how to get help. A pregnant neighbor had contractions two days ago. An ambulance was called, but got held up at an IDF checkpoint en route to the woman's home—a routine occurrence in the territories. Waiting for the ambulance to arrive, the woman only had her nervous husband to help her. By the time the medical team got there, all they had to do was cut the umbilical chord.

G's family deals in nylon and cloth tarpaulin. The renewed violence and prolonged curfew came at a time of peak business for them: the Jewish holiday of Sukkoth. From their home you can see their locked-up shop; above the entrance hangs a sign bearing the message "Happy Sukkoth." Now the family has no customers—neither Jews nor Arabs. Some customers owe them money, but, confined to his home, G has no way to collect the debts. "It's as if we are in Ansar 3," (a temporary prison set up in the Negev by the Israelis during the Intifada[1]) says one brother, and the other brother corrects him, "only there we were protected, and here we aren't. You can't go out on this street at all," he explains. "Behind us, in the market's alleys, children can poke their heads out and step into the street. Because settlers don't live there, and there aren't as many soldiers, so people can move around a little. But here we have a street which is constantly used by Jews, and so stepping outside is a question of life and death." When a settler walks alone in the street, Palestinians are less wary, even if the Jewish man is armed. But when settlers move in a pack and come across a local Palestinian resident who has dared to venture out, heaven help him.

We experienced this ominous Hebron dynamic last Friday. I have a press card, and M, a teacher by profession, and a refugee camp resident, has documentation from B'Tselem stating that he is a field researcher for the Israeli organization. It was not the first time M had entered an area under curfew. Though he never would have done so alone, without the company of an Israeli journalist. Even if IDF soldiers allow him to enter the area, Jewish settlers might hassle him. As it turned out, when we passed a group of settlers (pregnant women, infants in strollers, children roaming between policemen's legs and soldiers' rifles), a young man started to yell: "Arab, you're not allowed here, there's a curfew, get out of here!" As he shouted, he approached M, brandishing his fist and repeating the message, "Arab, get out of here, there's a curfew!" The soldiers and policemen made no effort to get the young settler to back off. Instead, they ordered M to move away. And so we did, under a torrent of jeers.

Jewish settlers in Hebron are protected by a dozen or more IDF posts, most of them set up on Palestinian rooftops. Armed settlers often climb up to these posts to join the soldiers, and monitor the scene. One such army post sits atop the home of Dr. Tyseer Zahada. For two years, the army operated an observation post above his house, on a street leading to the Tel Rumeida[2] settlement. After a lengthy struggle, the army finally dismantled it. Some years ago, Dr. Zahada established a maternity hospital on the first floor, and the army presence frightened away his patients. The army moved its post to an abandoned building nearby. But on October 1st, shortly after the Intifada erupted, soldiers returned to Dr. Zahada's building, breaking down the door, and re-erecting the post, this time as a shooting position. Once or twice, Zahada has seen soldiers carry ammunition crates up to the roof. Whenever they shoot, the whole house shakes. Once, a missile was also fired from the roof.

Despite the filth (soldiers' urine trickles down into the courtyard, food cans and wrappers are cast unto the balcony, and empty bullet cartridges mix with the children's Lego) and despite his run-ins with the soldiers (whom, he says, are especially vulgar), Dr. Zahada's real fear is of the settlers. At this point, he observes, the settlers appear content to "just" damage cars and windows, and push around pedestrians who dare to break the curfew. Like the woman whose daughter went out to buy some food when the curfew was lifted, but got caught outside when it was reinstated earlier than had been announced. Her mother went out to search for her. Dr. Zahada watched from his window as settlers pushed the mother around. A few days before this incident, he relays, some settlers ransacked his own home, entering the gated yard, where they shattered his potted plants. Dr. Zahada, who tends each plant lovingly, was horrified to think that his children could have been hurt by the hurled objects.

"We are confined to the house, and the soldiers do nothing to stop the settlers. They told me to hold on to the document that informs me that my roof has been seized—the one I refused to sign. I asked them, 'Why is it important?' and the officer said I could use it to complain should there be any damage. 'And where should I complain?' I asked him. 'At the Kiryat `Arba[3] police station,' he replied. So I asked them to tell me who on earth will hear my complaint there, and didn't bother to mention that no one ever compensated me for the damages incurred the last time they took over my roof."

It has been a month since the doctor worked. His clinic is deserted. The smell of lentil soup wafts out from the kitchen— "the poor man's meat" as the Arabic saying goes. Like everyone, he is eating into his savings. Last week was a holiday. His younger son rejoiced, "I'll get money from my uncles." His father was surprised; in the past it was he who gave money to his nephews. The son explained: "But you don't work anymore."

Stationed at one of the Old City's guard posts, two IDF soldiers admit that their job is not a pleasant one. Telling people that they cannot leave their homes is not much fun. But they do not let anyone outside, even when local residents beg for some leeway. As they see it, an order is an order. It is also not fun to be confined to your base in punishment for breaking orders. Besides, the soldiers explain, this is our country, and the Arabs have attacked us, and that's not right. On the Jewish Sabbath, the soldiers add, it's a little better. Settlers bring them all sorts of goodies. How is that, I ask, since (as was well publicized at the time) the army ordered soldiers not to accept foodstuffs from Hebron's settlers. "That's right," the soldiers confirm, "but then a new commander came, and rescinded the order." The IDF spokesman says that no such change of policy was instituted—soldiers stationed in Hebron are still forbidden to accept the settlers' treats.

---

1. The first Intifada of 1987–1992.

2. The ancient city of Hebron, where Abraham is said to have bargained for the cave he bought to bury his family, and where King David is said to have reigned before moving to Jerusalem. Today, a hill in the city of Hebron inhabited by Palestinians and a handful of Israeli settlers.

3. Israeli settlement northeast of Hebron, population: 8,000.

November 14, 2000

Following the Camp David summit, officials at the Orient House[1] decided to translate the proposals raised there into maps, to illustrate the Palestinians' objections to Ehud Barak's famous offer. "The Israeli team didn't draft maps," says Faisal Husseini, who heads the Palestinian team for negotiations on Jerusalem "so we did it ourselves; we prepared maps that will show the nature of the compromise offered there—the compromise that wasn't." The Israeli proposals—translated into maps—will be accompanied by maps depicting the Palestinian proposals for a solution. The Jerusalem Task Force, a professional team set up by Husseini in May 2000, is currently putting the finishing touches on these maps.

Husseini and his task force, headed by Dr. Manuel Hassassian of Bethlehem University, had intended to present the maps to their Israeli colleagues, the American brokers, and various European observers. The Palestinians, insists Husseini, honored the mutual commitment made at Camp David not to go to the media. "We had no interest in going public, we weren't looking for problems—we were looking for a solution." However, the outbreak of the Intifada, and the great surprise it generated among Israelis, prompted them to do just that, before the resumption of negotiations. The Palestinians hope that the relevant parties will finally understand why the Israeli proposals were neither generous nor conciliatory, but rather an attempt to divide the territory so as to preclude the possibility of establishing a viable Palestinian state.

After Camp David, says Husseini, his colleagues who were in contact with Israeli negotiators discovered that none of them had a real mandate to negotiate. Everything was in Barak's hands. Meanwhile, the 2000 Intifada broke out before negotiations resumed. World public opinion, says Husseini, "is hostage to the impression that a far-reaching Israeli compromise was made at Camp David, and does not understand what the Palestinians are so enraged about." Thus, it was decided to publicize the maps in order to explain the uprising, the anger, and the Palestinian claim that we are still subject to Israeli occupation—as a basis for resuming negotiations."

Dr. Hassassian says the Israelis were vague at Camp David. One time they spoke of annexing 5% of the West Bank, another time they spoke of annexing 10%. Sometimes the calculations were based on a "downsized" West Bank, excluding the no-man's-land of the 1949 armistice lines, or East Jerusalem, or the Dead Sea. Sometimes the calculations were based on the original area captured in 1967. Therefore, he explains, the maps are based on estimates of the proposals made at Camp David.

The question of Jerusalem is essential for understanding the Palestinian objection to Barak's proposals, says Husseini. Not because of its great religious significance, but because of its importance for guaranteeing Palestinian geographic continuity and viability. "Israel wants to determine the permanent borders based on the settlements. We say, the fate of the settlements will be determined by the borders." Husseini reiterates what has been clearly stated in almost every Palestinian platform, and what he believes to be the message of the Intifada today: The principle must be a return to the borders of June 4, 1967. The moment Israel accepts this principle, the Palestinians will be ready to negotiate its flexible implementation and the fate of the settlements: evacuation, territorial exchanges, granting Palestinian citizenship to settlers who wish to remain, etc. "Already at the Madrid Conference[2] we understood that negotiations were based on UN Resolutions 242 and 338," says Husseini. "The negotiations are not over the resolutions, but rather how to implement them."

According to Husseini, there is no contradiction between resuming negotiations and continuing the Intifada. "After all, in the end a solution will only be reached through negotiations. Israelis understand that they can negotiate while continuing to expand and build settlements. I understand that I can negotiate while the Intifada continues. Otherwise, Israel should stop all construction in the settlements immediately."

The Jerusalem Task Force works in coordination with the Palestinian negotiations department headed by Abu Mazen (Mahmoud Abbas), but drafting the maps was an independent initiative, clarifies Husseini. Jerusalem is under discussion and here, too, the key word is settlements. Therefore, he is convinced that his initiative affects the entire process. According to the data available to the task force, Palestinian built-up areas cover no more than 5% of the West Bank (including East Jerusalem), whereas the built-up areas of the settlements (including East Jerusalem) cover about 1.8% of the West Bank. These figures reflect both the scale of Israeli construction since 1967 and the curtailment of Palestinian development.

According to the Palestinians, the Israeli proposals at Camp David—translated into Orient House maps—perpetuated this principle: Jewish development and the establishment of Jerusalem as an Israeli metropolis on the one hand, and on the other hand, dividing the Palestinian communities from each other; pushing Palestinian Jerusalem to the geographic, political, and economic margins; and stunting the natural development of Bethlehem-Jerusalem-Ramallah into a Palestinian metropolis.

Had the Palestinians accepted the Israeli proposals for Jerusalem, which entailed annexing the Adumim bloc (120 square kilometers around the settlement of Ma`aleh Adumim) and the Etzion bloc, they would have, in essence, agreed to splitting the West Bank part of the Palestinian state in two: north and south, with passage between them falling under Israeli jurisdiction. The Israeli demand at Camp David to control two east-west routes as well—the Trans-Samaria highway and the Tel Aviv-Amman road (still in the planning stage)—would have meant that the West Bank part of the Palestinian state would be divided into three separate cantons, as the Palestinians put it, and the connection between them would always be at the mercy of Israel, the IDF, and the settlers.

1.PLO headquarters in East Jerusalem.

2. Multilateral peace negotiations held in 1991–1992.

November 20, 2000

You can find soldiers like him at any military post in the West Bank or Gaza. But we met in an Israeli city. He is the same age as many of those who are confronting the IDF. He is good-natured, shy but forthright, and tends to favor subjects in the humanities. Were he out of uniform, you might think he was on his way to India or South America.

"Every day, the regulations for opening fire change, sometimes several times a day," he says. "Every day before we go out they define the rules for opening fire. This varies from place to place. There are places where the regulations are more lenient. The orders are that we be very selective, very precise, and if we shoot, it's because we restrained ourselves enough. It also depends on the day. After the lynching,[1] for example, the regulations for opening fire were far more relaxed than they had been the day before. But usually the regulations call for restraint. There seems to be an impression that I am trigger-happy, but the opposite is true, I'm glad that the regulations are moderate."

Q: How do you know they are moderate? What are the criteria?

A: Sharpshooters are given precise orders for opening fire: people who throw Molotov cocktails can be shot in the legs, but people who pull out weapons can be shot head on.

Q: They give you video cameras?

A: They call them documentation kits, and see to it that every person killed is also photographed. The photo confirms that he was not under the age of 12, that he was holding a weapon.

Q: So, are the Palestinian figures false?

A: It's hard for me to say, but I can remember a few incidents when we definitely shot an adult, and over the radio they asked if we were sure we'd shot an adult, and we prayed that the soldier in charge of the kit had filmed it because they [the Palestinians] were already saying we'd shot a kid. It could be that they make incorrect statements, but there are also incidents where a child is killed because of a soldier's stupid mistake and I haven't heard them [the IDF] publicizing this afterwards.

Q: What is a mistake? That the rifle moves?

A: For example, someone says to the other forces that he has identified someone suspicious—we identified a boy who is making strange movements; maybe he wants to pick up a stone or something like that. The one who identified him requests permission to fire in his direction. The forward command, the brigade commander, definitely does not allow it, and he continues to plead, and so the commander says, "if you think he is very suspicious, fire a warning shot," and a warning shot is 20 meters, and into an open area. From the ensuing investigation, it turns out that he saw the person's head through a telescope, took five meters, and the wind... the rifle wasn't aimed right, and he hit him in the head.

Q: Do you know how many children have been killed?

A: No. If we ask, they tell us. And in some places they provide the figures without us asking.

Q: And do you know how many have been killed altogether?

A: No, I've heard various numbers in different places, but I wouldn't sign on them.

Q: And children?

84

A: I can't estimate at all the number of children who have been killed.

Q: How do you explain that people have been hit in the upper part of the body? Do you need special skill to be on target?

A: We shoot very selectively. We shoot whoever needs to be shot—or at least 90% of the time. That is to say, everyone who throws a Molotov cocktail and can kill someone else; if he's holding it—we shoot him. We don't fire at him with an automatic weapon, but with a sniper's rifle, and in most cases these aren't long ranges. A sniper, from 200 meters, has no problem hitting the head and certainly if he aims at the head—the upper part of the body—there's no problem. A Molotov cocktail endangers the soldiers in the jeeps, who are only 25 meters away.

A sniper is like a pilot, his work is very clean, safe—unless there are other snipers around, and then his work is very dangerous. The real danger for a sharpshooter is another sharpshooter, a Palestinian one. And they have them. There are even some who aren't bad. If you have the weapons and the sights, you already have a 50% chance [of hitting the target]. In this war the ranges are short. A sharpshooter's skill is measured at 500-600 meters—then he's a real sharpshooter.

Q: And when do you become skilled?

A: We, as sharpshooters, have taken good care to look—even though they haven't told us to—for places where there could be another sharpshooter: houses, windows—because this is what is really scary. What is also scary are the stray bullets. Their shooting is not well aimed. Though we are afraid of the Palestinian police. At the moment they act of their own accord, and they simply have better training. The *Tanzim* are untrained and sometimes when they report "exchanges of fire" on the radio we laugh.

The *Tanzim* aren't the Palestinian police. The police know how to shoot on target, and they have precise, reliable weapons.

I have to say that the IDF was ready for these disturbances. I remember that about two months before it all began, I wasn't thinking in this direction. I was happy and optimistic about Barak's election, about the fact that negotiations would proceed. Then we had a discussion with our commanders. They foresaw the disturbances. They told us that Arafat had learned from Israel that establishing a state by force and with many people killed is a positive thing because it imparts values: it strengthens the leader, gives the people ideals—esprit de corps—like we have after three wars, when seven armies attacked us. They expected that there would be something, only they didn't know whether it would be a war, disturbances, or demonstrations. They were hoping it would be demonstrations, but were prepared for the possibility that it would be a war. There are contingency plans that detail exactly what will happen if they decide to go ahead and reoccupy the territories we gave back, and set up a military regime like in the 1950s, or something like that. Of course this is terrible. Even I, a simple soldier, have heard about these plans.

Q: Do you remember how it all started?

A: My father got very angry with Sharon for visiting [the Temple Mount]. I just thought it was an ordinary event.

Q: Didn't you know that on that Friday, four people were killed at the mosque and another two near al-Muqassed Hospital?

A: No, I didn't. I think that after the first day, you become a soldier. On the first and last day [of service] you go back to being yourself—to your political opinions. In between you try to disconnect yourself. In my opinion, most of the Jewish settlements beyond the 1967 borders are not important. But at the moment, you are a defender and 100% a defender, and those people are very important to you. We, as Israelis, have to decide on a clear line because if we decide that we aren't giving back the settlements then we, the soldiers, will find it much easier to fight. At the moment I am sure that Arafat knows this too.

Q: Someone who is about to throw a Molotov cocktail is moving all the time, how do you aim when someone is in constant motion?

A: It depends on the distance. At 100 meters it's not hard, and we also practice this, and there are also easy targets—it all depends on the distance. At 500 meters you already know not to aim at the head but at mid-body, because it's easier, and you also have to take the wind into account, and the deviation factor. But at 100 meters it's almost sterile shooting, very easy. In Lebanon a sharpshooter had to be far more skilled, the distances were 700-1,000 meters.

Q: Is it easy to shoot at the head?

A: Yes. Their guys, including those who throw Molotov cocktails, or even shoot, have an instinct to stop, think a moment where to throw or shoot, and this moment gives the sniper five or six seconds, and it's no problem. If he stops, even if you are far away, hitting the head is no problem.

Q: Behind the Jeeps there is usually someone with a rifle. Isn't he a sharpshooter?

A: He usually shoots rubber bullets.

Q: And what kind do you shoot?

A: A sharpshooter fires a lethal bullet; a bullet bigger than an M-16, and its quality is superior to a submachine gun bullet.

Q: The Palestinians say that the IDF uses a high muzzle velocity. Is that what you do?

A: The muzzle velocity is not that high, less than that of an ordinary M-16. The question is how critical is this. A sniper's bullet kills if it hits the body. This is a bullet that is "full metal jacket"—cased entirely in metal. In a regular bullet, the bottom part isn't encased, and this interferes with its aerodynamics. The air eats the lead a bit on the part that isn't encased, the way air can eat at a mountain, and gradually it gets inside the bullet and distorts its direction. This doesn't happen with a sniper's bullet.

What is also important is the weapon itself, that nothing be attached to the muzzle. Ideally, next to every sharpshooter there is someone with binoculars who aims.

Q: Of course you can also see.

A: You see whether you've hit the person through the telescope, but you don't see exactly where the bullet went. A person whose job it is to aim can see this. Through regular binoculars you can see the reverberations the bullet leaves, the dust, the tin, and then he says that you hit at two o'clock, 60 centimeters next to the person. If a sniper isn't on target with the first bullet, with the second one it's almost a sure thing.

Q: Do they tell you to aim for the head, or is it up to you?

A: If they tell a sharpshooter to fire, his intention will be to hit the head because if a sniper shoots, he shoots to kill. Unless there is a specific individual—in this war it hasn't happened much—whom you're instructed to shoot in the legs, which they also ask sharpshooters to do.

Q: Why haven't there been?

A: There is a policy to only shoot people who are clearly endangering lives. This decreases the amount of shooting by the IDF and the number of wounded. Maybe it increases the number of dead. Meanwhile, the IDF is trying very hard not to shoot, not to kill, to let them demonstrate a bit—maybe because of what they told us about two months before it all started, to let Arafat have his demonstrations without giving him and the surrounding countries an excuse to go to war.

Q: Isn't there a danger that snipers will compete to see who does more shooting?

A: With us, there is no such thing. Somebody told me about one place, where the older guys were angry because the younger guys weren't restrained. They were hankering to shoot. But even I, who before the army said I would try very hard not to shoot... if you're already there and into your weapon and you go out on an ambush, it's terrible to say this, but you hope that something will come of it. You sit there at night and it's very boring and you're really tired, and your last hope is that you'll catch the bad guys and teach them a lesson.

In one place, the older guys arrived to replace us, and they couldn't believe how much the young guys were shooting. After they say: "Stop!" you have to stop shooting immediately. And it took them another minute, because of their craving to shoot. These are the kinds of things that, in my opinion, weaken the IDF—the lack of restraint. There are even soldiers who fire a rubber bullet but load a regular bullet ahead of it—it increases the force. It usually kills.

Q: Do you know about the investigation of errors?

A: Every IDF shot is reported and investigated.

Q: I've been in those places, those demonstrations, where the Palestinians open fire.

A: Are you trying to say that the Palestinian fire is pathetic?

Q: Yes.

A: I agree. Usually the Palestinian fire is pathetic.

Q: And the army knows it is pathetic.

A: Yes. The shooting is totally ridiculous. And when there's finally shooting, you know that most of it will be into the air.

Q: Are they just showing off?

A: Yes. The IDF knows this.

Q: So why kill, why not just injure?

A: If you decide to wound people, more people will get hurt, and the question is whether this is better. Wounding fuels the anger even more.

Q: Who told you so?

A: This is my opinion. That is, if you wound someone, even the process of getting hit, when he screams and says it hurts.

Q: I've seen a lot of funerals. They cry over the dead and then head for the roadblocks.

A: If the IDF goes for wounding people, more people will be hurt.

Q: So the number of wounded now isn't so high?

A: No.

Q: The IDF knew that when Fatah activists opened fire they were just showing off, and that their shooting should not be allowed to improve. Yet Palestinian shooting has improved, so what good has the escalatory response been?

A: I have a friend who is a settler, and for him the firing is not pathetic at all. In his opinion, every time they shoot, we have to fire back tenfold. If you were to talk with him, this conversation would be totally different. You are talking to me, and I ask myself more questions, like whether I should just let them shoot and maybe I shouldn't fire back. When I am a soldier I don't ask myself. I ask, but there are orders, and I know in advance that if they shoot, all I need to do is ask myself if I should shoot again. Mistakes happen because this is not how things go. One guy decides to shoot, and someone else decides to do the opposite. Now I'll be a bit tougher: the IDF shoots because there are instances when soldiers are killed.

Q: Is it in revenge?

A: I don't know whether the IDF takes revenge. But every time there's a serious incident, it's political, you can feel it; you know as a soldier that if in that day's papers they printed a lot of things that happened to the IDF, then they will let you shoot more; that on that night I am going to be shooting more than I did the night before.

Q: Because you want to, or because they let you?

A: Because they let me. I didn't want to shoot that much, though there are a lot of soldiers who do. At first I also wanted to shoot, and after I shot a few times I said, "enough."

Q: You haven't shot children.

A: None of the snipers have shot children.

Q: But nonetheless there are children who were wounded or killed after they were hit in the head. Unless these were mistakes.

A: If they were children, they were mistakes.

Q: Do they talk to you about this?

A: They talk to us about it a lot. They forbid us to shoot children.

Q: How do they say it?

A: You don't shoot a child who is 12 or younger.

Q: That is, shooting a child of 12 or older is permissible?

A: Twelve and up is allowed. He's not a child anymore, he's already had his bar mitzvah; something like that.

Q: Thirteen is bar mitzvah age.

A: Twelve and up you're allowed to shoot. That's what they tell us.

Q: Again: you're allowed to shoot children age 12 and up.

A: Because by definition it doesn't seem to me to be a child anymore, even though in the United States a child can be 23.

Q: Under international law, a child is defined as someone up to the age of 18.

A: Up to 18 is a child?

Q: So, according to the IDF, it is 12?

A: According to what the IDF tells its soldiers. I don't know if this is what the IDF tells the media.

Q: And children are below the age of 12. Is there no order that between 12-18 you shoot at the legs and not the head?

A: Of course we try to see to it that he is over 20.

Q: In the ten seconds that you have…

A: In the ten seconds that I have I must estimate how old he is.

Q: And where the wind is blowing, and what the margin of deviation is, and which way he'll jump…

A: Yes, but sharpshooters hardly make mistakes. The mistakes are made by people who aren't sharpshooters.

Q: And they happen to hit the children's heads, just by chance?

A: If you say you have seen a lot of children that have been hit in the head, then yes, it is sharpshooters.

Q: So what you're saying is that our definition of children is different.

A: Your definition is different.

Q: Because for you, it's someone who is no older than 12.

A: Yes.

Q: But a child of 13 doesn't bear arms no matter what you call him, a boy or a teenager or a man.

A: He may not hold a gun but he may hold a Molotov cocktail, and in some places it is permissible to shoot people who throw firebombs.

Q: Do you know how many people were killed yesterday?

A: No. Unfortunately.

Q: What do soldiers talk about among themselves?

A: We mostly exchange experiences and argue over whether this is all necessary or whether we should want to open fire or not.

Q: And there are those who want to open fire more.

A: Certainly.

Q: And the commanders say they can't, are they part of these conversations?

A: Who said the commanders don't think like them?

Q: From what you say about the caution regulating sharpshooters, I conclude that all the people who were killed were armed. But it doesn't look that way to me, and I am familiar with events in the field.

A: Nor does it look that way to me. There's nothing to be done, if the IDF decides that it is responding and reacting, a lot of mistakes will happen and, relatively speaking, a lot of people will be killed. On the other hand, a lot more could be getting killed.

Q: I have seen a pamphlet with regulations for opening fire.

A: There's no such thing, they don't hand them out at all. Everything is done in accordance with the orders the commander gives us that morning.

Q: I want to go back to the matter of the 12-year-olds. Who set this age?

A: I heard that it was important for the IDF to know whether someone was over 12, so I understood that 12 is the age where they draw the line. They didn't give us an age they just said that we shouldn't shoot children. The IDF doesn't specify ages. We take care not to kill, not to have incidents with too many dead. Six dead is normal, there could be a lot more.

Q: What do you mean by "normal"?

A: They shoot at us, and if someone shoots at you, even if it's pathetic, you have to shoot back.

In response to a query by *Ha'aretz*, the IDF spokesman would not name a specific age under which one is considered a child. Nor would he provide an estimate of how many children have been killed, and what their ages were. The spokesman did state that: "The soldiers open fire with live ammunition only in life threatening situations in accordance with their field commander's orders. When the clashes erupted these regulations were redefined with the intention of protecting IDF soldiers' lives… The Palestinian Authority and the terrorist organizations, which send children to the frontlines of clashes… are making cynical use of these children and endangering their lives. The IDF regrets the loss of life in general, and that of children in particular, but it must be remembered that those who does not want harm to come to their children, should not be sending them into the frontlines of a war zone."

1.An incident on October 12, 2000 when two IDF reserves soldiers entered Ramallah and were killed by a Palestinian mob.

December 20, 2000

At a meal breaking another day of fasting (where most of those seated around the table had, admittedly, not fasted), J related how his mother worries over him. He lives in Ramallah and she in Bir Zeit. One morning she heard on the news that a 50-year-old man with a heart problem experienced chest pains but the Palestinian ambulance transporting him to the hospital was detained at an IDF roadblock. Detained so long that he finally died. J's mother was frantic—she thought that her son was the subject of the newscast. She called his home, but he was not in. After calling "the entire world," J told the others, his mother finally got hold of him. "I was beside myself with worry," she told him, between sighs. "But, mother," he replied, "why did you think the person in question was me?" "The news report said that he had a heart problem." "But, mother, do you think that I am the only man in Palestine who has a heart problem?" "The newscaster said that he was 50." "But, mother, I am 51." "True, but you know how news reports are never accurate."

The IDF uses two kinds of roadblocks: the ordinary kind and another kind, which constitutes a permanent, large obstruction. The ordinary kind of roadblock consists of a few concrete or plastic blocks, with or without tire-piercers, and a handful of soldiers. Sometimes, after a great deal of pleading, or if a car bears diplomatic plates, the soldiers will allow free passage. The permanent, obstructive kind of roadblock is the "last word" in the IDF's tactics to suppress the Intifada. This obstruction is a simple, yet clever "improvement" that saves the IDF personnel resources. It often consists of a high earth rampart and a number of concrete blocks. In some cases, the rampart and the blocks are adjacent to one another, while in other cases the earth covers the blocks. Some road obstructions consist only of a deep ditch that an IDF bulldozer has dug across a side road leading to a main road, while others include both a ditch and concrete blocks. Of course, an IDF or Border Patrol jeep positioned near the obstruction with a rifle barrel sticking out of one of its windows ensures that no one will be foolish enough to bring a bulldozer to try to fill the ditch and clear away the blocks.

There are seven roads leading to and from Beit Jala[1] and western Bethlehem. All of these roads have been obstructed and are now closed to vehicular traffic. In other words, even if an extremely compassionate IDF soldier wanted to allow an ambulance transporting a heart patient to pass, he would have to first summon a bulldozer and some digging implements in order to clear the way.

The Tunnel Road junction and the highway to Betar `Illit[2] are clear of Palestinian cars. Residents of the villages west of Bethlehem—Nahalin, Batir, Wadi Fuqin, and Husan—take a taxi until they arrive at the obstruction set up on a road that, in any event, is intended for Palestinian use. A Border Patrol jeep ensures that taxi drivers do not park their vehicles too close to the obstruction and idle their motors 100 meters up the hill. The passengers—elderly persons, teenagers, women, children, healthy individuals, and people with medical conditions—must climb the earth rampart, descend the other side, continue descending the hill, traverse a field, cross Road number 60 (the Tunnel Road—a highway where cars speed accordingly), arrive safely on the other side, pass a Border Patrol jeep (from which personnel fire for no apparent reason), climb the earth rampart that blocks the road leading to and from the Palestinian village of al-Khader, empty their shoes of pebbles and dirt, and then board a taxi to Bethlehem.

The way back from Bethlehem involves the same distance— a few hundred meters—but is more demanding: it is uphill, and usually people are carrying baskets full of food bought in the region's failing commercial center, very often after a day of work or errands. One woman, who carries a basket of apples on her head, says, as she climbs the earth rampart: "It's too bad you weren't here two days ago. My daughter was just about to give birth, but the ambulance couldn't take her directly to the hospital. We had to carry her over the rampart as her water broke." Two youths support an elderly man, practically carrying him in their arms, especially when heading uphill. He is not their father; they simply traveled in the same taxi, which brought him back from a medical examination. One man carries a used oven uphill. Barely able to answer a single question, he replies: "70 kilos."

A three-year-old girl is being pulled along by her mother and aunt, both of whom carry baskets on their heads as well as their arms. She is frightened by the television camera; it looks like the rifle she saw a few moments earlier in the hands of one of the soldiers. A number of men arrive at the obstruction huffing and puffing, and one of them, without missing a beat, looks back and asks, "What kind of peace is this, anyway?" Answering his own question, he proclaims: "The peace of the brave, of course!" One young man initially says he has "some business to attend to in Bethlehem." However, a moment later, he cannot contain himself, and removes a small plastic bottle from his jacket pocket. "You see, this is milk—my wife's milk. She gave birth two days ago. Our baby girl is sick; she is hospitalized in Bethlehem. My wife is recuperating at home. Because of the road obstructions, she cannot take a car or an ambulance to the hospital. In her condition, she cannot walk this distance. So that is why I am bringing our baby my wife's milk."

---

1. Palestinian town west of Bethlehem, population: 12,000.
2. Jewish settlement in the southern West Bank, population: 17,000.

March 25, 2001

Recently, in the Saja`iya neighborhood in eastern Gaza, a group of 20 schoolchildren in their early teens got together. The children are devoted to the symbolic activism of the Intifada: throwing stones at well-fortified IDF positions, military jeeps, and settlers' cars on the road connecting Netzarim[1] to Israel. While most of these children's friends have come to see these symbolic acts as futile, and nowadays return home after school, this local group continues to head eastward, to the Karni-Muntar[2] crossing.

On February 26, a new IDF position was set up there, consisting of a concrete observation post, an armored personnel carrier (APC) and, on occasion, a military jeep or two. The entire area around the position is clear; hundreds of dunams of orchards have been razed, and any movement in the area is detectable by the soldiers.

The children from Saja`iya are well aware that the stones they throw, even with the help of a slingshot, barely scratch the post and the armored vehicles. The soldiers fire straight at them. The children know they may be injured or killed—that one or two boulders are not enough for all of them to take cover behind—yet they continue to come.

The adults around them have noted that recently these kids have become increasingly devout. They make sure to attend the funeral of every person killed by IDF fire and when they reach the cemetery, they rub their faces with earth as an act of purification before the prayers commence. Their devotion is understood as a way of coping with fear—the lot of every child and adult living in the Strip.

Local activists from the two rival Islamic movements—Hamas and Islamic Jihad—have tried to convince the kids to declare their affiliation with their respective organizations. The children reject the idea outright and stress that they are independent. Muhammad Hilis, 13, was a member of the group. On Tuesday,

February 27th he approached the border area where the Netzarim settlers pass by with a military escort. At around 2:30 pm, witnesses told a field researcher from the Palestinian Center for Human Rights, some 30 children congregated about 50 meters from the border with Israel and started throwing stones at the jeep leading the settlers' convoy. The jeep stopped and a soldier fired two live bullets at the kids. Hilis was hit on the left side of his head. Witnesses said the soldier did not try to warn the kids using non-lethal methods. Hilis died from his critical injury on March 1st.

But stone throwers are not the only ones hit with live ammunition. On the same Tuesday that Hilis was fatally injured, a bullet also hit five-year-old Fatma Abu Salah. Her family lives in the village of Absan, east of Khan Yunis, near the border with Israel. Her mother told the Gaza Center for Human Rights that shooting could be heard in the area as early as 4:30am. At 7:30am, Fatma was at the entrance to her kindergarten, about a kilometer west of the border. That is when she was shot. Was it a stray bullet from an exchange of fire? In Gaza they do not believe in stray bullets. People think that the IDF has equipment so advanced that they can see every target, day or night, and therefore, every shot fired, near or far, is intentional—even if it hits an eight-year-old boy.

Unlike Fatma Abu Salah, Mustafa al-Luka, 15, was shot from close range. A resident of the Brazil refugee quarter in Rafah, al-Luka was sitting in front of the al-Nur Mosque on February 26th at about 4:30pm when he heard some shots and an explosion. The mosque is located about ten meters from the Gaza-Egypt border and the median security road patrolled by Israel. He noticed an Israeli soldier peeking his head out of a tank driving along the border from west to east just as another tank approached from the east. The two tanks intersected opposite the mosque, he told the field researcher from the Palestinian Center for Human Rights. "I saw an Israeli soldier aiming his machine gun at me. I heard three shots. I felt something warm penetrating my right elbow and chest. I managed to run into the neighborhood and from there I was taken to Jeneina hospital (in Rafah)," he said.

Not a day goes by in Gaza without a number of children being injured by Israeli shooting and not a week goes by without at least one or two adults, or maybe one, two, or three children being killed in circumstances similar to those described above. People here experience the reports in the Israeli press about "easing regulations for opening fire" on their flesh. At first glance, it seems that people have accepted the fact that their lives are in constant danger because wherever they go they are within range of Israeli weapons. The expressions on people's faces, the jokes they make about the situation, and their ready smiles do not reveal fear or panic, and demonstrate an incredible ability to adapt to any situation, however insane.

That is why one Israeli reserve soldier, a psychotherapist serving at the Tel al-Sultan post, was so surprised to hear from Herve Landa, a fellow psychotherapist, that the Palestinians suffer emotionally from the daily barrage of machine gun, tank, helicopter, and rocket fire directed at their homes. "And I was sure the Palestinians don't experience any traumas or anxieties," said the Israeli soldier-psychotherapist. "They pass in front of us at the roadblock and their faces don't reveal any emotions." The two psychologists met by chance at one of the roadblocks in the Gaza Strip. The soldier wanted to know who the Frenchman was and what he was doing in such a dangerous place. So they started to chat.

Landa works for the French humanitarian organization Médecins Sans Frontières (MSF),[3] which was founded in 1972 to provide medical aid to people in places afflicted by wars, disasters, and bloody conflicts. In recent years, after gaining experience in places like Chechnya, Bosnia, and Kosovo, the organization realized that it is not enough to send medical teams to treat physical injuries, when emotional strains and their somatic manifestations are just as common and no less paralyzing. Given the renewed

Israeli-Palestinian conflict, MSF opened two new branches in the Palestinian territories—one in Gaza and one in the Old City of Hebron. Doctors and psychologists work together and in coordination with each other, exchanging information and using similar methods; they do not wait in clinics for people to come to them, but make house calls, mainly because of the restrictions on movement Israel has imposed on the Palestinians since October 2000. Palestinian interpreters who spent many years in Algeria assist them.

Families in the Khan Yunis refugee quarter, which is hemmed in from the west by IDF posts and the settlements of the Katif bloc, welcome Landa and his interpreter warmly. They sit in simple chairs in the courtyards of modest refugee homes, next to rooms destroyed by missiles or walls perforated by bullets, or on mattresses in guest rooms. Sometimes they talk to the entire family— parents and children alike—and sometimes they ask to speak with one family member in private. As Landa speaks and listens, he looks straight into their eyes, as if they shared a common language. He remembers every detail told him in previous meetings. He remembers who this child fought with after being shot in the leg by Israeli soldiers, and what that girl dreamt of after having a bullet lodged near her heart and no one expected her to survive—yet here she is, still alive. People are amazed that he remembers everything, which seems to be part of the treatment: the sense that someone is interested in what they have to say.

Palestinians are not accustomed to having intimate conversations. No one needs a foreign psychologist to know that daily death, so many wounded people and destroyed homes, and so much shelling and shooting, affect people's emotional states; that because of it, parents have trouble getting out of bed in the morning and children are more violent at school and wet their beds at night. But Landa is a great believer in the power of talking things through and the importance of digging beneath their fears and physical symptoms. It seems that Palestinian girls agree with him, and are far more open and eager to speak, even about deep emotions and bad dreams. It is much harder to get the boys to talk. Landa believes that thanks to the talks they have had, K, who has a bullet lodged near her heart, started getting out of bed after many long weeks, and began to smile again. She was injured inside her own home, by shots fired from a helicopter hovering over the neighborhood.

K lives in constant fear that the bullet will move and she will die. A dull pain next to her heart serves as a constant reminder of her injury. She is afraid to exert herself. She does not carry textbooks and notebooks to school. Landa suggests that she start by carrying one book at a time. She bakes just eight pitas, while her sisters bake dozens and half-jokingly reproach her for not doing her share of the housework. Before she met Landa, she did not bake a single pita. "People help themselves through me," he says. K relates a dream: the Jews are shooting at us; half of the people die half the people live. "Who are you with?" Landa asks. K is confused by the question. "Are you among the living or among the dead?" he asks again, and she remembers that not only did she stay alive, she helped with the rescue efforts. The dream is not a good one, she rules, and Landa tells her that he thinks it is a positive dream, because she is active in it and does everything she can.

A, who was hit in the leg and hip with live ammunition while throwing stones at soldiers, has noticed that since he was injured he is prone to fits of rage where he scares people away. When he hears shooting, his wound throbs and irritates him. By talking with Landa, he learns not to be afraid of the pain, to accept himself even when he has outbursts, and to admit that his friends are not to blame so that next time he will count quietly to himself before lashing out at them.

Landa tries to talk to the adults and the children about the fear they experience. If the fear strikes when they hear shots being fired, it is only natural. If the fear strikes when there is no shooting, they try to identify what triggers it. Many people told him that they are especially afraid at night. In many refugee homes, the bathroom is in the courtyard. The houses sit in full view of the Israeli observation towers. They are scared that if they move through the courtyard or turn on a light, they will be shot at. The parents, he notices, have trouble getting up in the morning because it is hard to find a reason. They are short-tempered with their children to cover up the helplessness they feel; without any income they cannot provide for their children, nor can they protect them from the gunfire.

In the evenings, when the shooting starts, the great exodus from the houses begins. Entire neighborhoods empty out at night. During the flight, someone always stays behind or gets lost and the trauma affects the family for days to come. The most serious symptom of anxiety is pain in the legs. People have discovered that their legs tremble uncontrollably, and are too weak to carry them. Talking with Landa helps them to understand that this is a logical outcome of their stress, and not the result of some mysterious incurable ailment.

In February, MSF's doctors and psychologist dealt with a particularly difficult case involving a mixture of physical and emotional injuries. On February 12th and 13th, the IDF used tear gas to disperse Palestinian demonstrators near Tufah Gate, at the end of the seaside road linking the center of Khan Yunis to its satellite refugee camp. Instead of the grayish white clouds, which the residents are accustomed to, a yellow and black gas spread through the neighborhood. People initially thought that something was burning and instead of running away from the smoke, they moved closer to its source. People vomited for several days, suffered abdominal pains, had tremors in their hands and legs and were unable to move. A tempest arose when some Palestinians, led by Yasser Arafat, suggested that Israel was using a banned poisonous gas. The IDF was quick to deny the charge.

Helen Briso, one of MSF's doctors, spent several days in the Khan Yunis hospital examining the patients. Contrary to Israeli claims that the tremors and other symptoms were staged; she confirmed that all of the physiological reactions were genuine. MSF representatives concluded that the gas used by the IDF was indeed in very high concentrations, which the people were not used to. Most of the Palestinian doctors reached the same conclusion and some of them also acknowledged that the ongoing physical symptoms were a kind of hysteria caused by the unfamiliar gas. Landa encountered people who were convinced that the gas would cause cancer. M, K's older sister, was hospitalized for several days, unable to move. "I'd rather be injured by gunfire, than inhale tear gas again," she says repeatedly.

In the schools, guidance counselors speak with the children and teachers are instructed to listen to their concerns. Nevertheless, Q, a teacher at a school in Rafah, wonders whether the heart-to-heart conversations do any good, when the surrounding circumstances—the cause for the traumas—stay the same. Q's eldest son, 12-year-old Basel, thinks every day about his friend who was killed. Every corner in the crowded refugee camp reminds him of their games. When he fights with his mother, he says: "I'll go to the border, a Jew will shoot me, and I'll die." And Q asks, as do many Palestinian parents and teachers, what can she do? What can she possibly do, when every day children continue to be wounded and killed? According to many Palestinians, everyone simply adapts, or gets used to the fear, or ceases to be afraid.

Q has a hard time answering her students' questions. One girl in her class who lives near the border—a place that attracts IDF fire—was hit in her back with live ammunition. "Didn't the soldier know that I just went out to get some bread?" she asks her teacher again and again. And another wounded boy keeps asking the adults in his neighborhood whether the Jews have no children—if that is why "they shoot at us indiscriminately."

1. Israeli settlement in the central Gaza Strip, population: 300.

2. Point of entry and exit to and from the Gaza Strip barred to Palestinians.

3. Doctors Without Borders.

PART THREE

(2001)

"Why would we need a key when we don't have a house?"

July 30, 2001

In July 2000, Dr. Saleh Abdel Jawad, a political science professor from Bir Zeit University, wondered what was wrong with
his forecasts. In February 2000 he sensed that Palestinian society was on the verge of blowing up. He just couldn't say
whether this was going to be a blow-up against Israel or a dou-
ble fit of rage—against Israel and the Palestinian Authority
(PA). He did not anticipate that half a year would go by without "the pressure cooker exploding."

During the year preceding the al-Aqsa Intifada, many
Palestinians talked of an imminent explosion. These predictions were not based on secret information about contingency
plans (supposedly) being prepared by the PA. On the contrary,
those issuing the warnings believed that the eruption would be
spontaneous and its timing and pretext impossible to foresee—
just like the first Intifada.

When it erupted, everybody supported the new Intifada. But
the way it has developed and is being conducted raises many
questions, and much frustration. A gap has emerged between
broad support for the need to rise up, and discomfort over the
forms the uprising has taken. Saleh Abdel Jawad is among the
academics working to narrow this gap, with limited success.

The predictions of eruption made by Abdel Jawad and others were based on their analysis of the Palestinian public's general discontentment with the Oslo process. Most Palestinians,
says Abdel Jawad, supported the process as a means to independence and the establishment of a state within the 1967 borders. "In this respect, the Palestinian silent majority is in the
peace camp." But their frustration stemmed from what became
increasingly clear as the process was implemented: "Israel,
instead of gradually withdrawing and loosening its hold on the
Palestinian people and territories, tightened its grip."

In addition to lack of faith in Israel's intentions, anger also accumulated against the PA, for two reasons. First, because it failed to adequately handle—on the political and diplomatic levels—what Palestinians perceived as Israel's intentional foot-dragging in carrying out the withdrawal. Second, because the PA's system of governance lacked the rule of law, was built around its security apparatus, and created wealth for its officials at a time when most of the people suffered ongoing economic distress. Therefore, "Israeli intelligence claims that Arafat planned the Intifada are both false and misconceived," says Abdel Jawad. On the contrary, Palestinian society criticizes the PA for not planning enough—in the last few years and since the Intifada began—and only reacting to Israeli moves.

Indeed, when things finally exploded, the PA did not try to stop it, because it was also fed up with Israeli policy. However, they expected a short-lived outburst. In Abdel Jawad's estimation, Arafat hoped to improve the Palestinian position at the negotiating table with the pressure of a popular uprising.

The possibility that popular rage would also be directed at the PA was there all along. But Israel, with its escalation tactics, very quickly "succeeded" in eliminating it and strengthening the PA's public standing instead. "The death of so many demonstrators in the first ten days of the Intifada gave public legitimacy to the imperative of using the arms at the PA's disposal (by its security personnel and Fatah activists). Moreover, Israel chose to target PA buildings early on. On the day of the lynching in Ramallah,[1] October 12th, Israel bombarded PA facilities throughout the West Bank and Gaza. [By] striking at the PA [Israel] restored the [Palestinian] public's faith in it, which it had lost several years prior." Nevertheless, Abdel Jawad says, the public is still waiting for internal changes in the PA's system of governance. There are those who believe, and Abdel Jawad is among them, that reform is a pre-condition for the successful continuation of the struggle against the occupation.

The speed at which the Intifada turned from a popular uprising into a series of shooting incidents, armed clashes, and terror attacks did not surprise Abdel Jawad. "Both nations, the Israeli and the Palestinian, have a similar rhetoric: they believe that the other side only understands the language of force. People felt that the first Intifada, which was for the most part unarmed, did not yield the desired political results. The successful struggle waged by the Hizballah against Israel in Lebanon strengthened this feeling. A second reason [for the militarization of the Intifada] is the dangerous overabundance of weapons among Palestinians. A lot of arms have been acquired on an individual basis in recent years. Even before the Intifada, internal struggles started to degenerate into armed conflicts, because of the proliferation of arms.

"A third reason for the militarization of the Intifada is the geographic reconfiguration that took place under Oslo. Today, there are fewer points of friction between soldiers and civilians, and these are concentrated around the roadblocks. This has rendered the stone a more symbolic and less effective 'weapon' than ever, and cut off the majority of the public from the occupation's representatives—the soldiers. This has made way for weapons that can actually reach the soldiers."

Abdel Jawad points to the reciprocal relationship between armed Palestinian activists and the IDF. During the first weeks of the al-Aqsa Intifada, Palestinian shooting was "in the air," or "at the moon"—shooting that cannot, or perhaps does not, intend to hit anyone. Shooting that is, from a Palestinian perspective, ineffective. Abdel Jawad thinks the IDF understood the significance of this ceremonial and declarative shooting perfectly, but chose to respond to it as if it were shooting between equal forces. "The exaggeration of the significance of this shooting created the illusion that there was a real armed conflict going on. Thus, despite public anger over shooting from residential areas, the shooters' aura as fighters grew. That is, the people who fired from residential areas helped the IDF to escalate things, and with its retaliatory actions the IDF strengthened the [Palestinian] line of thinking that only the use of arms can cause the Israelis real losses."

This type of struggle necessarily neutralizes most of the population and becomes the domain of small groups. In this context, remarks Abdel Jawad, and in the context of the closure, blockade, and encirclement—which affect the entire population—it is possible to explain widespread Palestinian support for suicide bombings inside Israel. However, Abdel Jawad, who in the past has written and spoken out against terror attacks inside Israel, believes that this support is not deeply rooted in Palestinian society, and can easily change.

However, if conscious changes in the Intifada are desired, there is a need for public discussion, which, Abdel Jawad says, hardly exists in Palestinian society. Here and there articles have been published in the Palestinian press criticizing the way the Intifada is going: its militarization, the shooting from residential areas, and a number of pieces condemning the brutality of the lynching and the murder of Jews who happen into Palestinian towns. Similar things can be heard at public gatherings. But they have not stimulated broad discussion or reached their desired targets: senior PA officials, Fatah activists, and armed militants. The absence of public debate over the way the Intifada is being conducted, morally and practically, frustrates Abdel Jawad. Nonetheless, he can list a number of reasons for this. The Palestinians have known years of censorship by military and/or authoritarian regimes—from the British Mandate, through the periods of Jordanian rule and Israeli occupation, to the Palestinian Authority. Coupled with the structural limitations of a clan-based society, it has proven difficult to develop a tradition of open debate, and whoever has dared to speak out has suffered for it.

Another factor at work is the lack of solidarity in this Intifada, compared to the first one. Perhaps this is because the people expected the Palestinian Authority to take the place of the spontaneous group initiatives of the past. Perhaps this is because economic and attitudinal chasms have deepened in the past seven years, and a new alienating element has been introduced: the degree to which one enjoys PA patronage. Perhaps it is because active resistance to the occupation is no longer a mass, popular experience, though "Israel punishes the entire population with its oppressive measures." In any case, Abdel Jawad admits that neither he nor his colleagues have contact with the residents of the refugee camps—from which many of the armed activists come. "There haven't been serious attempts to bring academics and people from the camps together to discuss the questions that concern us all, such as how to improve the struggle against the occupation."

Abdel Jawad feels that academics who try to stimulate debate are regarded with suspicion: "They accuse us of not suffering like the rest while allowing ourselves to criticize what is taking place. But social criticism has value in and of itself, regardless of the critic's individual experience. Furthermore, it is true that, relatively speaking, materially speaking, we suffer less. But Israeli oppression affects everyone. We are also under siege, we are also subject to shelling and bombardment, we also fear for our children."

He draws a connection between the absence of a culture of public debate and the fact that "on both sides, the Israeli and the Palestinian, there are no leaders who can outright say 'no' to their people." Only Faisal Husseini, says Abdel Jawad with longing, was such a leader. He recalls two joint Israeli-Palestinian events, one in 1988 and one in 1989, at which it was decided that neither Israeli nor Palestinian flags would be waved. At both events Palestinian youths raised the Palestinian flag, contrary to what had been agreed. It was Husseini who went up to them and firmly demanded that they take it down.

Saleh Abdel Jawad laments the fact that during the Oslo period the Palestinian leadership did not say outright to its people that this was not a victory agreement but an agreement stemming from weakness and defeat. Secretly, they fulfilled their various commitments to the Israelis, while concealing the agreement's shortcomings to their own public. This tradition of concealment also interferes with the culture of public criticism, the essence of which is the open discussion of weakness and defeat, without it being understood as "unpatriotic." And the result: among themselves many people talk about faults and failings, but their voices have yet to form a significant social force capable of bringing about meaningful change.

---

1. An incident when two IDF reserves soldiers entered the city and were killed by a Palestinian mob.

August 15, 2001

In the framework of the war the Palestinians have declared on us, these are the weapons at their disposal: demonstrations at IDF roadblocks and in urban centers; commercial strikes; calls to boycott Israeli products; stolen Israeli cars; leaflets; stones—used by the masses mostly in the first few weeks; Molotov cocktails; guns; rifles; machine guns; mortar shells; explosive devices; hand grenades; and "live" bombs—meaning suicide-bombers.

The Palestinian security positions along the invisible borders separating Palestinian territories from Israeli-controlled areas (including Jewish settlements) are: concrete structures, sandbags, and tin shacks. The Palestinians who continue to throw stones and Molotov cocktails hide behind the frames of wrecked cars, barrels, billboards, or house walls. Palestinians ambush Israeli soldiers and civilians with gunfire from orchards, hills, empty buildings, and refugee camp hovels. In this way, Palestinians have injured and killed Israeli soldiers as well as Israeli civilians traveling in non-armored cars. Palestinians practice drive-by shooting. They have cells whose members plant explosive devices in the dead of night on highways used by IDF and settler vehicles. They fire on Gilo[1] as well as Neve Dekalim[2] and Psagot.[3] Palestinians have murdered Israelis who have entered the areas controlled by the Palestinian Authority (PA). One Palestinian fatally ran over soldiers and civilians standing at an official "give a soldier a lift" station. Another Palestinian shot at soldiers outside the Ministry of Defense in Tel Aviv. Explosive devices and car bombs have been planted in Israel. About a dozen Palestinians have carried out suicide-bombings in Israeli towns and dozens more are waiting in line to do the same. More than 150 Israelis have been killed including women, children, and the elderly.

In Israel's defensive war against this Palestinian offensive, these are the weapons at the disposal of the IDF, whose troops are deployed throughout the West Bank and Gaza— where some three million Palestinians live: F-16 fighter-jets; helicopter gun-ships; pilotless drones; tanks; armored personnel carriers; armored jeeps; reinforced concrete positions on highways and junctions; observation towers; ships; sniper rifles; bulldozers; bombs; tank and mortar shells; air-to-ground and ground-to-ground missiles; tear-gas and stun grenades; barbed-wire; collaborators. The IDF fires from the air, sea, and ground; from tanks; from fortified positions; from observation towers; from behind jeeps.

Throughout the West Bank and Gaza, the IDF has bases opposite Palestinian refugee neighborhoods, between cities and villages, and within Jewish settlements. Tanks and armored vehicles travel by the light of day along highways, and are stationed atop hills, in settlements, or by the roadside.

This is what Israel does with the weapons it possesses and the means of control it exercises: assassinates Palestinians whom the General Security Services (GSS)[4] claim are linked to terrorist attacks against Israelis both inside the green line or beyond it; kills and wounds dozens of armed Palestinians; kills hundreds and wounds thousands of unarmed Palestinians including women, children, and the elderly; demolishes houses with bulldozers and tanks; demolishes Palestinian police or security personnel positions; shells buildings belonging to the PA; seizes homes located along highways; uproots orchards and fields; destroys hothouses, factories, and workshops; detains more than 1,000 Palestinians; imposes curfews for days and weeks on entire neighborhoods or villages located near settlements; imposes closure on the entire West Bank and Gaza Strip; denies Palestinians access to international crossing points; creates physical obstructions: concrete blocks, trenches, and earth ramparts to prevent Palestinian vehicles from traveling from one place to another; blocks main highways in the West Bank and Gaza to Palestinian vehicular traffic; beats Palestinian pedestrians; halts traffic on "Palestinian" roads for hours on end; prevents beach access to the residents (including children) of Rafah and Khan Yunis; limits the importation of food, medicines, and raw materials into the Palestinian territories; limits the marketing of Palestinian agricultural produce; issues evacuation and demolition orders on homes in areas adjacent to the green line; reduces the offshore territory in which Gazan fishing boats can operate from 12 nautical miles to three.

Despite this, the Palestinians carry on: some demonstrate; some fire weapons; some plant bombs; and some dispatch suicide-bombers. All circumvent IDF roadblocks on foot. Some stay home and get shelled nightly or hide in stairwells because there are no air-raid shelters. Some live in tents because their homes have been demolished. All Palestinian children hide

under the bed or heavy blankets when Israeli fighter jets or helicopter gun-ships fly over their homes. The PA arrests and holds
lightning trials for those suspected of collaborating with Israel.
Many slip into Israel to earn some money. Some slip into Israel
to blow themselves up.

---

1. Israeli settlement in southeast Jerusalem considered by Israel to be a "neighborhood"
in annexed East Jerusalem.

2. Israeli settlement in the southern Gaza Strip, population: 2,500.

3. Israeli settlement east of Ramallah, population: 1,000.

4. Also known by its Hebrew acronym as the *Shin Bet* or *Shabak.*

August 20, 2001

Palestinians traveling along the roads of the Gaza Strip rarely see
an Israeli soldier. Expanses of upturned gray soil and dry thorns
extend outward from either side of the road. Over the past ten
months, the IDF has uprooted thousands of olive, citrus, and
palm trees as well as grapevines, obliterating hundreds of
dunams of fields and hothouses. Soldiers are invisible in this
wasteland fashioned by army bulldozers. What is visible are
concrete blocks bisecting roads to separate Israeli from
Palestinian traffic, as well as tanks, armored personnel carriers
(APCs), armored jeeps, observation towers equipped with video
cameras, positions dug into small hills covered by camouflage
nets, and guard posts.

The guard posts—round concrete structures of varying
height—have largely replaced the tanks, which at the beginning
of the Intifada could be seen at every major intersection. Rifle
and machine-gun barrels protrude from the narrow slits that
ring these guard posts. Sometimes a hand can be seen sticking
out of a slit: a soldier directing a car to stop or keep moving.

Equally invisible are the soldiers who man the positions just steps away from the dense residential quarters of Khan Yunis and Rafah.

"As far as I could see, the bulldozer that destroyed my house could have been operated by remote control," says Anwar Kalloub from "Block O"—a refugee neighborhood in Rafah, adjacent to the Egyptian border. On the night of July 10th, he watched as an enormous tractor ("It wasn't a tractor, it was a building that moves") chewed up and spat out his home until it was reduced to a pile of rubble. He could not see who was operating the tractor. "A 15-year-old dream was destroyed in a matter of seconds; money I'd saved up from 20 years of work evaporated in a single night." Sixteen residential homes were demolished that night, in what the IDF described as "engineering activity and the removal of abandoned buildings, from which individuals emerged to lay explosives and from which shots were fired at IDF soldiers." All together, about 50 homes have been demolished in Rafah, which has a population of about 100,000. Another 1,000 dwellings have been damaged by gunfire, mortar shells, or fires set off by incendiary illumination shells. The windows of several hundred more homes have been shattered by the concussion of shooting and shelling. Life in Rafah goes on in the shadow of unseen soldiers, APCs rumbling along the Egyptian border, and reinforced positions filled with weaponry of every sort; between the homes of the dead and injured, beside destroyed houses, within dwellings perforated by bullets, and amid an unemployment rate of more than 60%.

Anwar Kalloub sits with other owners of demolished houses, at the still-intact home of a neighbor. Together they look at the piles of rubble: a shattered and overturned refrigerator, a school backpack, a few scattered Lego blocks, torn school notebooks, shreds of furniture, twisted iron rods. "Are these abandoned homes?" Kalloub asks rhetorically. He requests that the guests not get any closer to what had been his home. From his experience, and that of his neighbor, when anyone approaches the border, the invisible soldiers start shooting from the nearby post. Kalloub's home stood a few meters from the border fence. Part of it was built in 1948, the rest in 1996. Anwar and his brother Jihad recently bought it from its previous owner. Originally, their family came from Ashdod.[1] Kalloub, 38, has worked for the same vendor in Tel Aviv's Carmel market for 20 years. He would rehire Kalloub whenever the protracted closures and curfews of the first Intifada were lifted. The two men speak on the phone occasionally. Kalloub still owes him a few hundred shekels, which he borrowed last year. Don't worry about the money, his boss tells him. You'll pay it back when you return to work. For the past nine months he has not been able to go to work—a job for which he used to leave home every morning at 1:30am and return at 9:00pm.

Kalloub paid $17,000 for the house next to the border, a sizable sum in a city that has the highest poverty rate in the Strip. Unpaved sandy paths ring the houses like in most of the city's refugee neighborhoods. A closed sewage system was completed only two months ago replacing the open sewer canals. The Kalloub family paid for the house on September 2, 2000. Its proximity to the border didn't bother them, "Who thought at the time that the Israelis would shoot incessantly from their bunkers along the borders and destroy people's homes?" They moved into the house on October 10th, a few days after the Intifada began. "Who thought it would go on so long? And anyway, where else could we live?" On October 18th, the army fired at the neighborhood, including the Kalloub house, for the first time. The IDF Spokesman said it was in response to Palestinian gunfire. Altogether the house was fired upon five times. On two occasions, the family was at home. They crowded into a room on the side furthest from the border fence.

"The soldiers definitely knew there were children in the house," says Kalloub. The video camera on the observation tower on the other side of the fence—meters from their front door—undoubtedly captured them as they came in and out of the house.

Subsequently, when the exchanges of gunfire and mortar shells grew more frequent, the family rented a tiny flat in central Rafah. But when their money ran out, they had no choice but to come back to the house along the border. They comforted themselves by saying that things were calmer now, that there was less shooting, that the armed youths were no longer going around the neighborhood trying to "tickle" the well-fortified position with a few bullets, attempts which were invariably met with a barrage of IDF fire and shelling.

According to Kalloub and neighbors living in houses that have not been destroyed but which now form the front line facing the border, the soldiers have fired from the post and APCs on countless occasions when not a single Palestinian shot was fired at them. "We thought we were going to die twice a day, whenever a tank passed along the fence," which is reinforced with concrete and sand banks. At such times, the neighborhood would tremble in fear from the rumbling of the APCs. (Generally Palestinians do not differentiate between tanks and APCs, but according to Israel's agreement with Egypt, the IDF may not place tanks along the border.) Kalloub points to a concrete pillar leaning sideways over a mound of rubble. It was a support column in Muhammad Abu Libda's house—of which all that remains is a decorated metal door in its frame. Now the door opens unto a pile of broken concrete, asbestos siding, and home appliances. Before the house was demolished, the woman of the house sat under the column and kneaded dough. Suddenly a shot fired from the post hit the column about 30cm from the woman's head.

On July 10th, just after midnight, Kalloub was chatting with some friends in the street when he heard the APCs coming. He ran home just in time to see the bulldozers and to wake his wife and six children, as well as his neighbor, Abu Khalil. He noticed that the man had not emerged from his house before the bulldozer had starting chomping at it. It was only then that the exchange of gunfire started. Armed Palestinians ran to the scene and fired at the force, which responded in kind. "Should we take the key?" asked one of Kalloub's daughters. He stared at her, dazed. "Why would we need a key when we don't have a house?" he replied. His parents still hold the large iron key to their house in Ashdod.

The Palestinian Authority (PA) promised Kalloub and a few dozen others alternate housing. Each family was allotted a 150 square meter parcel of land, on which UNWRA[2] would build them a home. Each family also received 8,000 NIS in exchange for waiving its rights to the land on which their ruined home stood. Abu Khalil, an elderly refugee from Beer Sheba, refused to sign the waiver, or accept the money. He does not want to be a refugee for a second time, he says.

"Block O" is situated on the north side of Saladin Street, a commercial thoroughfare that used to run straight into the Egyptian part of Rafah, and from there to al-Arish. Saladin was considered the Champs-Elysees of Rafah. It was brightly lit, bustling—a magnet for shoppers and merchants alike. After the Sinai was returned to Egypt, its popularity declined. But today, one needs a special brand of courage, or total resignation to one's fate, to walk down the street in the direction of the border. All of the shops along a 200-meter stretch inward from the border are closed. Their metal doors, perforated with countless holes of every size, attest to the bullets and shells they have absorbed. Holes also perforate the walls of all the houses still standing within a 100-500 meter range of the border, on both sides of the street. This is true for the refugee neighborhoods as well as the area just south of Saladin Street—the older residential quarters. These are the original neighborhoods of pre-1948 Rafah, many of whose residents belong to the large Kishta clan.

During a guided tour of one of their homes, they point to the perforated walls, which have been patched with cement. Look, there are eight holes in the children's room. In the older aunt's room—nine holes. In the northern room—a large hole carved out by a shell that had to be sealed with cinder blocks. Cautiously, they open the back door of the house. More piles of rubble come into view. Some of the homes were demolished on April 14th, others on July 19th. Here and there a yellow chrysanthemum grows in the debris. And looming over the entire scene is the IDF position, with its observation tower and video camera. Here, too, they caution visitors against walking around the rubble, lest someone open fire from the position or a tank concealed behind the concrete fence and sand bank. The narrow spaces between the houses have been filled with sand bags to try and minimize the available target surfaces.

The Kishta family is cautious for good reason. The wife of one of the brothers was seriously injured while cooking in the kitchen of her home, which is located in the fourth or fifth row of houses from the border. Shrapnel from a shell intended for somewhere else hit her. She lost an eye, and is now paralyzed in one arm and both legs. She is hospitalized in Saudi Arabia, with 90% disability. In November, Najib, one of the brothers, was walking home from a field belonging to the family. It is situated in an open expanse between the fourth and fifth rows of houses. An IDF bullet penetrated the narrow metal grating under one of the houses and hit him in the head. He was one of the first residents of Rafah to be killed in this Intifada.

Shadi Siam, 17, was killed on May 24th. Siam supported himself through odd jobs in carpentry or agriculture. He was deaf, and did not hear the gunfire that day as he was walking near

Saladin Street. He had been walking with friends, but something caught his attention and he fell behind. When they heard gunshots, his friends motioned to him to lie down and take cover, but it was too late. He was hit in the chest by a bullet that went through his back. The school for the deaf that Siam attended only two years prior suspended classes for three days after he was killed. The teachers held special sessions with the agitated students, and discussed ways that the deaf might avoid gunfire in the future. Siam's killing triggered special awareness of the problems facing Rafah's deaf, when invisible soldiers shoot from observation towers, tanks, and outposts. Rafah has an especially high incidence of deafness: the older families tend to intermarry, so as to keep the land in the family. These marriages often result in children with hearing impairments. Ten years ago, the Rafah community decided to build a special school for them. No one thought they would need special training on what to do when a civilian population comes under incessant fire.

------

1. Isdud in Arabic; a Palestinian village northeast of Gaza occupied and depopulated by Israeli forces in October 1948. Most of the village was destroyed. Many of Isdud's 5,000 refugees and their descendents now live in the Gaza Strip. The Jewish port city of Ashdod was established in its vicinity.

2. United Nations Relief and Works Agency.

September 11, 2001

[...] Last Wednesday, IDF officers serving in the West Bank took part in a full-day seminar on "human dignity": more precisely, the behavior of the soldiers at the roadblocks. During the lectures and the ensuing discussions, the initiators of the seminar stressed that the roadblocks are a security necessity—a preventative operational task of unquestionable importance. However, they said, at the same time they are convinced that steps must be taken to end the harassment and humiliation that occur at the roadblocks. In their estimation, different behavior on the part of the soldiers will decrease feelings of frustration, anger, and bitterness among Palestinians. Dr. Danny Stetman, a professor of philosophy at Haifa University and Shlomo Politis, the legal adviser to the IDF in the West Bank were invited to lecture to about 20 commanders. I, too, was invited to speak before this forum.

About three hours after the IDF seminar, Fatah activists in the Deheisheh Refugee Camp related how they simply do not leave the Bethlehem area. All men in their 40s, they do not want to gamble with the unpredictable moods of the soldiers at the road-blocks. The latter can check and find out that each and every one of them spent some time in Israeli prisons before the Oslo Accords, and decide that he is a dangerous person who must be detained. This conversation took place in the rooftop restaurant of the Ibda`a cultural center in the camp, established as a grassroots refugee initiative by some local activists. Afterwards, as we descended the stairs, one of the activists pointed to a large lecture hall. At its end, near the blackboard, sat a group of people study-ing. The teacher was journalist Nasser Laham. Twelve people—ten men and two women—study Hebrew with Laham, who picked up the language in prison years ago while serving a six-year sen-tence for activism in the Popular Front for the Liberation of Palestine (PFLP). The subject of today's lesson: roadblocks.

There are those who study Hebrew because they work in Jerusalem. Every morning they have to elude soldiers just to arrive at their steady jobs without the required permits. One of them is studying Hebrew because he was hospitalized for nine months in Jerusalem. He began to speak Hebrew there, and wants to contin-ue. Another comes all the way from Jerusalem, where she lives, despite the roadblocks. Were she to attend a course in West Jerusalem people would harass her—she wears traditional Islamic attire. And besides, Laham is such a good teacher. There is also a Palestinian security officer in the group, with his radio equipment turned on. He is an optimist: he thinks that the days of security coordination will return and he will need the Hebrew. Another student does not even know how to write properly in Arabic. But says he knows that he will need Hebrew even more. "I'm studying Hebrew in order to live," says another student. When Israeli forces invaded Beit Jala, they did not make it to the lesson. But when there is "routine" shooting and exchanges of fire, they never miss a class.

The students try to replicate in Hebrew the stories they make up in order to persuade the soldiers to let them through. "That is, you lie," says Laham, writing the three-letter root of the verb "to lie"—*shin-kuf-resh*—on the board, noting that, like Arabic, the Hebrew language is based on roots. The students say, "of course we lie," and switch to Arabic: "The soldiers will never let us through if we tell them that we need to go to work." Each of them tried at one time to tell the truth. "So go to Yasser Arafat and let him pay your salary," they hear repeatedly in all sorts of variations. They listen, jot down the words they don't know, and ask Laham their meanings. What is *maskoret* (salary), and what is *tahat* (ass) from the order *shev al hatahat* (sit on your ass). And what is *yetush* (mosquito). There are soldiers who like to call the people who go through the roadblocks names. The students write down what they hear and together have translated about 200 expressions: "You're so small," "Get lost," "Don't meddle," "Germs," "Filthy," "Hands up," "Stand there," "Turn off the engine," "Move back," "Scram," "Liar," "I don't believe you," "Tell the truth," "Stupid," "I'll break your legs," "I'll slash your tires." At the roadblocks, a soldier can often be heard asking people: "Decide what you want—a shot that is worth $2,000 from Iraq"—a reference to the donation given to families of Palestinians who are killed, or "*khaber a`ajel*"—a "breaking news" item broadcast on local television every time the IDF opens fire and injures people.

In Hebrew, which fast lapses back into Arabic, they relate difficult experiences like that of a bridegroom who was traveling to his own wedding through Wadi Nar.[1] The soldiers at the roadblock noticed his outfit, and asked him why he was dressed that way. He told them. "So what will you say if we keep you here for an hour?" they asked. "Nothing," he said. "And two hours?" Also nothing. "And three?" Here he went silent. When they reached "Seven?" he said he would kill himself. Finally, they detained him for about four hours.

Laham writes a few words on the blackboard: "hour," "clock," "girls," and next to them some numbers. When the students find it difficult to conjugate the numbers in the plural, he discusses the shared origins of Hebrew and Arabic. "They are twin languages," say what you will about the conflict. He explains that the Hebrew that most of them know is roadblock Hebrew—violent, full of curses, ugly. In the same breath he tells his students: "I'm not religious, but don't forget that this is the language the Bible was written in. For believers, this is a language that has come down from God. Therefore it will exist forever."

After the lesson, Laham rushes to the local Bethlehem television station. There, every evening, he presents one of its most popular programs: "Journey to the Israeli Press." He translates items published in the newspapers, summarizes reports broadcast on Hebrew newscasts, and here and there offers his own commentary. That is, as long as the newspapers arrive from Jerusalem—a seven-minute car ride. There is a worker who sneaks around the roadblock every evening and brings them to him. When the worker is caught, there are no newspapers, and then a message appears on the screen: "The program will not be broadcast this evening due to technical difficulties."

---

1. Literally "Valley of Fire" in Arabic. A perilous hilly road east of Jerusalem that enables Palestinians without permits to enter Jerusalem to travel between the northern and southern West Bank.

October 17, 2001

The Palestinian Authority (PA) sent a harsh message to its people last week when its police opened fire on Palestinian civilians. The message was: when there is renewed contact between the PA and the bastion of Western democracy, the United States, together with a return to the negotiating table, forget about basic civil liberties such as the right to assemble, demonstrate, express an oppositional stance, or report on events. And no, there is also no guarantee that your authorities will respect your basic right to life. Israel and the United States expressed satisfaction with the message, as if the Palestinian police had gunned down dangerous terrorists on their way to murder Jews, rather than a group of demonstrators and passers-by, including a 13-year-old boy.

What would have happened if, on Monday ten days ago, the several hundred Hamas supporting students from the Islamic University in Gaza had continued their march to the plaza outside the Palestinian Legislative Council, carrying placards against the US attack on Afghanistan and holding up pictures of Osama bin Laden for the television cameras? There is no doubt that in the United States, but especially in Israel, it would have been argued that this was the ultimate proof that "the entire Palestinian nation" supports terrorism.

The PA could have responded that it cannot forsake civil liberties. Just as there are demonstrations against the attack on Afghanistan in the United States and Europe, as well as Israeli demonstrations against reaching an agreement with the Palestinians, the Palestinians, too, have the right to express views that are displeasing to the American government. The PA's role, their talented spokespersons might have explained, is to prevent the creation of a "parallel authority"—one that tries to use force and the threat of suicide bombings to impose a policy different than that advanced by the official leadership.

At the same time, these talented spokespersons could have pointed to various polls that show that most of the Palestinian public does not support the terror attacks on the United States. They could say that the expression of support for bin Laden is regrettable but does not reflect the entire public, and launch an educational campaign to prove to the public that bin Laden is bad for the Palestinians.

The Palestinian Authority and its Chairman, Yasser Arafat, were elected in January 1996 for a term that was supposed to end with the interim period, that is, in May 1999. The interim period, however, was extended, as were the terms of office of the elected PA officials. As long as no new date is set for elections, it means, in effect, an open-ended extension of their terms in office. True, in the West and in Israel there is no expectation that Arab regimes be democratic. But the Palestinian public does expect this, and wants to develop a political culture based on democratic values, the rule of law, and respect for civil and human rights. With their terms of office extended indefinitely, members of the Palestinian leadership should be particularly sensitive to the public. But in practice, the opposite is true.

From the outset, the Intifada was aimed in two directions: the Israeli occupation and the Palestinian Authority. Many Palestinians see a direct link between the dysfunctional, disrespectful, and indeed, corrupt conduct of PA institutions and officials, the fact that years of negotiations with Israel have not brought them any closer to independence, the ongoing settlement enterprise, and the fact that the IDF continues to control most of the territories. People believe that a different kind of regime—one which consults, exchanges views, considers the positions of others, and in which everyone is equal before the law, would have strengthened the Palestinian negotiators vis-à-vis their Israeli colleagues, cum rivals.

Behind the three Gazan families whose sons were shot dead by the Palestinian police, stand large clans (especially the Abu Smallah family in Khan Yunis). Behind these large clans stand other families who share the same origins in the villages of Yibne and Beit Daras.[1] When citizens feel abandoned by their authorities, they seek cover in their basic communities: the clan, the village, the political organization, which, during the Israeli occupation, sometimes served as a surrogate clan in dealing with its members' needs. The violent dispersal of the demonstrators from the Islamic University sent the students of al-Azhar (affiliated with the PA and Fatah), the students of the Teachers College (also affiliated with the PA, though many of its students apparently support Hamas), and students from numerous other schools—into the streets. A public not necessarily affiliated with Hamas was, thus, pushed into a common front with it against the PA.

The shooting of demonstrators put all of the political organizations—from Fatah (the backbone of support for a peace agreement with Israel) to Hamas—on a collision course with the Palestinian police. To break this front, stand up to the families who are threatening a blood feud in revenge for the wrongful death of their sons, and keep the Israelis and Americans satisfied, the PA will have to step up its repression. This will further blur the distinction between legitimate criticism, and the forceful imposition of an agenda by militias—who were not elected by anyone.

---

1. Palestinian villages occupied and depopulated by Israeli forces in June and July 1948, respectively, and subsequently destroyed. Many of Yibne's 5,000 refugees and their descendents now live in Rafah in the southern Gaza Strip, in a refugee neighborhood called "Yibne," which has been subject to numerous military attacks and house-demolition campaigns by the Israeli army during the current uprising. Many of Beit Daras' 2,800 refugees and their descendents also live in Rafah.

December 10, 2001

International scoop: prima facie evidence indicates that there is support from Norway for Palestinian terrorist activity. And also from Germany, Switzerland, and Sweden.

On the night between Wednesday and Thursday last week, an IDF unit raided the Palestinian Central Bureau of Statistics (PCBS) in north al-Bireh. The announcement by the IDF spokesman stated that the raid was undertaken "in the framework of the IDF's fight against terror," and that in searches carried out at the bureau "of the Palestinian Authority... evidence was discovered that indicates prima facie that the PA supports terrorist activities. Among the evidence were documents showing transfers of money to the Palestinian Authority, filled out checkbooks, video cassettes, and computer disks."

The countries mentioned above funded the establishment of the bureau in 1994, as well as most of its research projects, surveys, and the census it conducted of all the residents of the Gaza Strip and West Bank (including East Jerusalem). The European Union also donated money to the bureau, $4 million, as part of the donor countries' support for the development of Palestinian civil institutions. Norway donated about $7 million; Germany $5 million; Switzerland $4 million; and Sweden, $1.5 million.

During its first five years of operation, all of the bureau's activities were funded by European donations. In 1999 and 2000, the PA covered 30% of its budget, and the rest was covered by contributions. In 2001, the year of the Intifada and the siege, its research projects were once again funded in full by donations. This is just one indication of the importance attributed in Europe to civil institutions like the PCBS. Every Palestinian, Israeli, or international study on Palestinian society inevitably makes use of its reliable data, updated reports, and comprehensive surveys, which shed light on various aspects of Palestinian society—such as leisure habits among children, child labor, women's work, women's health, and the decline in the standard of living due to the Intifada.

At what level of the military echelon was it decided to storm the building at 11pm on December 5th and raid every room on all five of its stories until 5am the next day? Presumably it was not the decision of the commander of the local force that has, since last Monday, and for the second time in two months, taken control of northern al-Bireh. Was it the General Security Services (GSS) that proposed the raid, with the hope of finding secret information in the databases of the bureau, which is responsible for the PA's population registry and voters' rosters? Was this a local interpretation of the political echelon's instruction to strike the PA, which has been declared a "supporter of terror," or was the bureau defined as an intelligence target in some political-military forum?

Perhaps the bureau was not chosen as an intelligence target but rather as a symbolic target? As the occupying power, Israel controlled all of the statistical data on Palestinian society—publicizing or hiding figures at will. Occupation is not merely the presence of soldiers and tanks, but also the control of information, its development, its application, and the dialogue that develops between it and the society it refers to. The PCBS took away one of Israel's means of control. Perhaps someone wanted to signal that the very preparation of an infrastructure for Palestinian independence is being targeted?

The raid on the PCBS left no impression in Israel. Nor, of course, did all the doors that were forced open and broken, the cabinets and desks whose contents were emptied onto the floor, the careful account books that were carted away along with computer hard drives and disks, or the two safes that were cracked (the IDF says no money was found in them; the bureau's director, Dr. Hassan Abu-Libdeh, says there was cash and it was taken). Nor the CDs that someone smashed, among them a disc that was the gift of the Israeli Central Bureau of Statistics: The 2001 Statistical Abstract of Israel. Nor the vulgarities that someone scrawled in Arabic on one of the documents (The IDF spokesman says that these claims are "not known").

The IDF knows that everyone will stand at attention upon hearing the "scientific" statement that "evidence has been found indicating prima facie support by the Palestinian Authority for terrorist activity." The need to combat terror and prevent devastating attacks is obvious. The problem is that it silences any independent public questioning of the nature of the targets the IDF, upon instructions from the government, chooses in order to combat terror. In Israel, they prefer to ignore the social and intellectual effort the Palestinians have made to develop an infrastructure for civil advancement. They refuse to see that only the prospect for human, social, and communal development will isolate terror.

For the time being, only one twisted logic is operative: the PA has been declared a supporter of terror, and every one of its institutions—civil and security—is suspected of supporting terror, and therefore, any accounting transaction, transfer of funds, check issued, or piece of data gathered—serve terror. If this is the case, does the fact that the United States government gave the Palestinian Central Bureau of Statistics $350,000 also make it, prima facie, a supporter of Palestinian terror?

December 17, 2002

Al-Tirah is a neighborhood of "puppies"—Palestinian yuppies, says one of its residents, mocking himself and his neighbors. With its high concentration of academics, Bir Zeit University professors, renowned journalists, doctors, lawyers etc., southwest Ramallah has flourished in recent years and boasts many villas, low-rise apartment complexes, and high-end stylish housing projects. The latter are scattered among olive groves, agricultural terraces, bougainvillea and jasmine plants, and private garages. There are also a couple of buildings, which do not appear to be meant for "puppies." And it is here, on the second floor of one of them, in a not especially large apartment, that Marwan Barghouti, leader of the Fatah in the West Bank, and his family, live.

Last Thursday morning, a few hours after a bus heading for the West Bank settlement of Emmanuel was ambushed, the IDF took over part of al-Tirah. They entered from the direction of the police station, which stood at the bottom of the hill until an F-16 fighter jet destroyed it a few months ago. Palestinian policemen have long stopped sleeping in their stations for fear of Israeli bombings. Instead, they camp out in nearby groves and orchards. The policemen, sleeping in their tents near the station when the IDF entered, managed to escape. When the soldiers came through, all they found was laundry hanging in the trees. Between 6am and 7am, a curfew was placed on al-Tirah, but only strictly enforced after 10am when IDF soldiers took up positions inside people's homes. In S's home they met resistance: S speaks fluent Hebrew and told them that there was no way they were going to turn her house into an army post. A, her husband, joined in and said the same in English. "I'll go to the press," he warned. "Go to Ariel Sharon for all I care," a soldier retorted. But it seems the Hebrew intimidated them and they left to invade someone else's home instead.

At midday, there was a knock on the Barghouti's door. Marwan Barghouti has not lived at home for the last year as a security precaution. Nor was he there on Thursday, even though it was a few days before 'Id al-Fitr, the holiday culminating the month of Ramadan. The day before, his brother and sister-in-law had arrived from Saudi Arabia for a visit. His wife, Fadwa, opened the door and saw a "battalion" of soldiers on her doorstep. "Whose house is this?" she was asked. "Marwan Barghouti's," she answered, prompting a meaningful "ah-ha" in response. "Thirty or forty soldiers entered the apartment," she said in an interview on Friday. "Some had photo cameras and others video cameras and they photographed everything, in every room, from every angle. The children started to cry, maybe because they had never seen so many soldiers and weapons at once. The soldiers did not ask to see identity cards. They informed us that we were allowed to remain in one of the three bedrooms, while they would inhabit the other rooms because 'we have to stay with you for a couple of days, that's a military decision.'"

According to Barghouti, an attorney by profession, they did not show her a seizure order. Nonetheless, they spread out in the living room, the stairwell, the kitchen, and the balcony. Sandbags were brought in and placed on the balcony, and an Israeli flag was draped outside. "That is your house and ours is here," the soldiers told her, explaining the division of the house to its owner. "Have you paid rent to divide up my flat?" Barghouti asked, not expecting an answer.

Military sources say that the house was occupied for purely operational reasons and there was never any intention of arresting Marwan Barghouti. The IDF spokesman says that the inhabitants can stay in the house, or leave if they so wish. "At first they made us all stay in one room," said Fadwa, "me, the four children, Rani the nanny, my brother- and sister-in-law." Eventually, they allowed the children to enter their rooms.

Initially, they forbade them from doing anything: don't go near the window, don't open it, don't move. Then they let the children stand in the hall that separates the bedrooms from the rest of the apartment and watch television, to help pass the time and diminish the fear, but with the sound muted, so as not to disturb the soldiers sleeping in the living room. None of the soldiers slept on the couch, she said. Only in sleeping bags, on the carpet. A large sniper's rifle was placed inside the living room, next to the balcony door. When it was time for the meal marking the end of another day of fasting, the soldiers prohibited the family from eating together in the kitchen. The nanny was allowed to prepare the meal, and each child was allowed into the kitchen to eat in turn, before being sent back to his room to make way for the next child.

Meanwhile, journalists began gathering outside. The soldiers in armored vehicles posted at the entrance to the building did not allow reporters to enter and observe what was taking place. When the number of cameras multiplied, one of the soldiers took down the Israeli flag. On Thursday, the soldiers prohibited relatives from visiting. On Friday, they allowed the neighbors' children to come in and play with their friends, jailed in their own home. Around 15 soldiers stayed in the house, Barghouti estimates. Three or four stood guard, while the rest slept soundly.

"Of course it's comfortable," she said, "instead of sleeping in tents outside, they have a ready-made, cozy apartment. We, on the other hand, couldn't sleep all night. But our experience is just an aspect of what's going on here, and it is not a question of food or personal discomfort. This is but one example of how the army can come into any Palestinian home and seize it as its own. Our right of ownership is not recognized under occupation."

On Friday morning, the IDF allowed Fadwa Barghouti to come out of her apartment to be interviewed by *Ha'aretz*.

Visiting the apartment was not permitted. Barghouti was given a special promise that she would be allowed to return to her home, confirming her version of events that when the IDF entered the house, family members were forbidden to leave if they had any intention of returning. "We allowed them to leave the apartment," one soldier told *Ha'aretz*, "but not to return," said Barghouti, completing the soldier's sentence. For Fadwa Barghouti, the interview was a chance to stretch out a bit. She sat on a rock opposite the soldiers. "Even if they arrested Marwan or assassinated him, what would they achieve? What have they achieved with all their assassinations and bombings? Only escalation," she said.

She pointed at the soldiers guarding her house and asked rhetorically, "Why do they think Barghouti became the so-called "leader of the Intifada?" After years of doing everything he could to convince his people that Oslo was the only way to independence and a state? Because he was left with nothing to convince them, or himself—given the construction in the settlements, the division of the territories into areas A, B and C, the redeployments that never came, the army that remained everywhere. "Marwan was elected, not appointed," she continued, "but even if he told the people who elected him to stop the struggle, they wouldn't listen to him. They will only listen if he can promise that something will come of it: a plan for full [Israeli] withdrawal to the 1967 lines."

During the conversation, an army commander came up to check that "everything is okay." In response to a question concerning the logic of setting up a military post on the second floor of a five-storey building, he said that he did not have permission to be interviewed. And no one can visit the apartment because that's the policy. But half an hour later, along came the deputy brigade commander who announced that one may indeed visit the apartment, if accompanied by soldiers. For 10 minutes. A surprise awaited Barghouti back at the apartment: while she was being interviewed downstairs, her family was allowed into the living room to watch television. One of the soldiers sat next to the children on a chair. The sandbags had been removed from the balcony to the stairwell. The sniper rifle had been moved and placed in a darkened room, which held other weapons and military equipment. The deputy brigade commander stressed that this was his first visit to the position, and that he had to point out to the soldiers that it was unsafe to set up a sniper's rifle in a room where children are running around.

A curious four-year-old boy, a neighbor's child, touched one of the soldiers' rifles. The soldier moved the insistent child's hand away with a smile. Suddenly, two relatives who had been denied entry the day before appeared. "The youngest boy embraced me as if I had come to visit him in prison," noted one relative, wiping tears from her eyes. To the soldiers she said, "This is a Muslim household. It is not customary for strange men to enter a house full of women and sleep among them. If you respect our faith you must leave!" The deputy brigade commander clarified that the relatives had been allowed to enter by mistake; the soldiers thought they were accompanying the journalist. He told the relatives to leave. "You leave! It's our home," insisted the brother-in-law. The deputy brigade commander said that it is not nice to take advantage of the fact that a reporter is in the house, and that conclusions will be drawn.

At 5pm Friday afternoon, 29 hours after the Barghouti apartment was overrun, the IDF soldiers picked up and left for another building. Military sources say that IDF officers sat with Barghouti to clarify that nothing was damaged and nothing was taken.

December 20, 2001

A, a resident of one of the housing projects in the al-Balu`a neighborhood of Ramallah, which the IDF occupied 17 days ago, "missed out" the first time the IDF captured his area: he was in Gaza, doing something related to his work with the Palestinian Authority, and got stuck there for over three weeks.

That is why the tanks that rumble past his window are a novelty for him. His children have long ceased to scrutinize every approaching tank, to examine the angle of its cannon, to study the difference between armored personnel carriers (APC) and tanks, and to recognize the soldiers that peek out from them. They only note that this time around, the soldiers are not as strict and rude. Perhaps because they have grown used to the neighborhood and realize that nobody is going to shoot at them. Perhaps because the curfew has been lifted "until further notice" and the soldiers are no longer obliged to enforce impossible orders on hundreds of elderly women and men, young girls and boys, schoolchildren, and clerks who pass through the neighborhood en route to Ramallah. And perhaps because the IDF plans to remain in Ramallah and al-Bireh for a while, so the soldiers have been told to show restraint and remember that they are, after all, positioned in a residential area.

In any event, in the first days, when the curfew was still in effect, A ran to the window, curious to see what was happening outside. Seated on a red armchair in his small, well-heated living room, he relays, mostly in pantomime: "The tank approached, and stopped just under the window. A soldier's head appeared. The soldier, wearing glasses, stared at me. And I stared back. Then he lifted his hand and made a "V" sign— victory. I told the kids to make a "V" sign back, but they were too shy or scared, and refused."

So A took matters into his own hands. He made a sweeping gesture meaning "No." "You?" he pointed at the soldier, "V?" he asked, making the two-digit sign. "No!!!" he shook his head and waved his hands in negation. "We," he said pointing to himself, "V," he said making the sign. The soldier opposite him gave him the finger. A, who could have been the soldier's father or older brother, continued with this didactic communication, ignoring the vulgar gesture: "You," he pointed at the soldier, "in the tank," he pointed at the tank, "what do you do?" he moved his hands as if turning a steering wheel, and then raised his shoulders in question. "No," responded the soldier with a shake of the head, and then disappeared into the tank and reappeared holding what looked to A like a bomb. A lifted his arms to the heavens in question, and turned his head to the side with the hope that the soldier will understand, "But isn't it a shame?" The soldier understood, because he too raised his hands as if to say, "But what can I do?"

The next day, the tank returned along with the soldier. It stopped outside A's window, and the soldier emerged. This time he waved to A and smiled. A returned the gesture, smiling back. Since then, it has become family lore: When a tank stops under the window they know it's the same soldier, whom the children, like to call *Abu Nadarat* (four eyes). On the third or fourth "visit," the soldier, with hand gestures as usual, asked if he could photograph the family peeking from the window. "What do I care," replied A with a shrug. The soldier disappeared into the tank, reemerged with a camera, and photographed the family.

Al-Yahoud[1] to most children and many adults means soldiers and army. "Dad," asked the three-year-old Damir (Conscience in Arabic), "Are the Jews born like us, little babies, or are they born already big with uniforms and guns?"

---

1. Arabic for "The Jews."

Amira Hass

PART FOUR

(2002)

"Mother, mother, what kind of war is this?"

January 16, 2002

On Friday a bus got stuck in the mud somewhere between Morag, a Gaza settlement, and Rafah on an unmarked dirt road that winds between fields and orchards, hothouses and stone houses, scattered across the farmland. It is more a track than a road—carved out after the IDF blocked the main road between Khan Yunis and Rafah a day earlier.

A long line of cars got held up behind the bus. Gradually, the drivers and male passengers got out to help push the bus. Two youths began speaking with the only woman who emerged from a car. The two said they were from the Tufah neighborhood in the Khan Yunis Refugee Camp (where the IDF has demolished dozens of homes in the past year) and that they are in the Palestinian coast guard. Then came the inevitable question, does she speak Hebrew? And completely naturally, even before her professional identity became known, they proceeded to chat with the Israeli woman, answering her questions about their lives, and asking her their own questions about hers. The conversation ended only because the bus was finally freed from the mud.

Hundreds of Israelis who would like to have similar experiences could, were it not for the Israeli army, which bars them from entering Area A—territories under Palestinian security and civil control. "Security imperatives" and the need to save lives, sound very convincing. Palestinians have murdered several Israelis who entered Area A to shop or dine in Palestinian towns. Regrettably, another Israeli was murdered yesterday near Beit Sahour.[1] Other Israelis on innocent trips were kidnapped and it took intervention and pressure to secure their release. But there are three comments that have to be made in response to these ostensibly reasonable arguments:

1. About 200,000 Israelis risk their lives every day when they drive on West Bank and Gaza roads to reach their homes in the settlements. The IDF does not prohibit them from risking their lives and the lives of their children. Quite the contrary, young soldiers are sent to risk their lives to protect the settlers. Meanwhile, three million Palestinians live in a regime of closure, curfew, and siege, allegedly to prevent any breach in the settlers' security.

2. Tens of thousands of young Israelis risk their lives every year by traveling to "exotic," dangerous places around the world. They climb snowcapped mountains, hike through jungles, and visit drug-infested islands. No government authority would dare prohibit them from tempting fate with their adventures.

3. The all-encompassing ban on entering Area A does not really stop those who want to buy a cheap sofa or some hashish. But it does curtail hundreds, perhaps thousands, of Israelis who are fed up with the patronizing filter through which the IDF passes its recycled, chewed-up, one-sided statements to the Israeli press. These are Israelis who are prepared to take the risk and are convinced that it is their moral and civic duty to monitor first-hand what their government and army are up to.

If these people could get into Area A and Gaza, they could come home and enlarge the circle of Israelis who are willing to hear something other than the IDF's version of reality. They would observe, and then explain, the real balance of power: who is threatened and who is doing the threatening. They would see dozens of tanks (each weighing more than 50 tons) perched on hilltops overlooking neighborhoods. They would see people forced to hike through valleys. They would see the armored guard posts with machine gun barrels poking out of every crack, and they would see the countless observation towers surrounding Palestinian villages and towns. They would see the torched fields and orchards the IDF leaves behind. They would go to places where dozens of Palestinian children have been killed and realize that no child throwing a stone or even a Molotov cocktail could possibly endanger the lives of the soldiers positioned there. They would hear, maybe even witness, soldiers shooting at civilians, shots that never make it into the IDF spokesman's reports. They would see how the West Bank and Gaza have turned into a terrain of fortresses and outposts, whose only purpose is to protect the settlements.

These Israelis would go in peacefully and leave peacefully, and they would bring out proof that the mythical fear of all Palestinians is not only groundless, but also promulgated for propaganda purposes.

More than anything, the ban on entering areas under Palestinian control enables the IDF to control the Israeli perception of reality. It allows the government to postpone, indefinitely, the moment at which the people will refuse to accept the logic of its policies. Unfortunately, the High Court of Justice cooperated with the army and the executive branch last week when it rejected a petition by three Members of Knesset from Hadash[2] to force the IDF to allow them into Gaza. Surely their safety was not at risk. But as the justices wrote, "public order" may have been disrupted. In other words, the ease with which the army and the government bombard the public with a distorted picture of reality.

1. Palestinian town east of Bethlehem.

2. The Democratic Front for Peace and Equality.

January 23, 2002

Demonstrations in Ramallah, even when held in the shadow of Israeli cannon barrels, have turned into social gatherings—an opportunity to exchange information and opinions on political developments. Marwan Barghouti usually participates in these rallies, even when there are explicit Israeli threats on his life. "I'm short, so I can hide behind you," he jokes to whoever expresses concern for his safety.

At one of these demonstrations, he started speaking in Hebrew with an Israeli woman who was present. Nearby, a PLO man of relatively high standing in the Palestinian Authority (PA), who returned to the territories with the "Tunis people" after 30 years in exile, muttered something under his breath about the Hebrew conversation. Barghouti continued chattering in the sister language. "Those who came from outside," he explained, "don't know Hebrew. They're *Goyim*."[1]

Barghouti is not the only Palestinian whose world of associations has been colored by Israeli-Jewish lore. There's a whole generation of people aged 30-50 who were born or raised in the territories and came to know Israel quite well. Some worked in Israel, others were active in the resistance against the occupation and were sentenced to long terms in Israeli jails. In prison, they learned about Israel through the wardens, the Israeli criminals, and their families. At work they met Israelis, heard about their troubles, and shared in their family celebrations. For every prison guard who embittered their lives, they remember the one who offered them a piece of cake baked by his wife. For every employer who fired them without paying their wages, they remember the one who sent money during a curfew or a siege.

They learned that Israel is a multi-dimensional society. It is impossible to exaggerate the importance of this experience, and what they gained from it, if one wants to understand the support that Barghouti's generation gave to the Madrid and Oslo processes. True, the Palestinian interpretation of those processes turned out to be different from the Israeli one. Barghouti and his comrades (and part of the Israeli peace camp) understood that they would lead to the establishment of a Palestinian state in the territories occupied in 1967, including East Jerusalem. The right of return, they believed, would be partially implemented, because as one of them said, "Having recognized Israel, we don't intend to undermine its existence as a Jewish state."

But they also expected Israel to acknowledge its responsibility for the Palestinian catastrophe of 1948, and they did not expect Israel to accelerate the rate of Jewish settlement in the territories.

Arafat may be a one-man ruler, who knew how to maneuver the entire PLO into accepting Oslo, but he could not have done so without the authentic support of Barghouti's generation for a two-state solution. Indeed, the peace process provided Fatah's leadership with a relative comfort that the rest of the Palestinian public was denied. But that was not why they supported Oslo. At most, this relative comfort kept them from responding in time to the ongoing construction in the settlements, the Civil Administration's prohibitions against Palestinian building, and the policy of closure—which affected every Palestinian.

Throughout the Oslo years, Barghouti and his generation— apparently under orders from Arafat—did what they could to keep a lid on popular unrest. But in September 2000, they joined the sub-currents of social and political anger. They came to the conclusion that polite negotiations with Israel over an end to the occupation were going nowhere.

Barghouti's generation listened to the youths who went to throw stones at the symbols of the occupation: armored jeeps, checkpoints, outposts. Many of these youths were shot dead. Barghouti and his colleagues may not have properly calculated the Israeli military response. They did not know how to stop the phenomenon of "shooting in the air" in time—what gave the IDF the justification to use unprecedented lethal force in the first week of the Intifada. In response to the destruction and massive number of casualties, the Fatah encouraged "effective fire" from the Palestinian point of view. In other words, against soldiers and settlers. Usually, his generation managed to convince the Fatah youth to stay inside the "'67 territories." The fact that the suicide attack in Hadera[2] was carried out by a Fatah man does not indicate a change in their approach. Nor does it prove that it was carried out with orders from above (as Israeli intelligence sources have insisted).

It only proves that a new generation of Fatah activists has come of age. One that does not know Israel the way Barghouti and his colleagues do. This is a generation that lost its childhood in the first Intifada, and its adolescence was truncated by the suffocating closures of Oslo. It may not yet be the generation that makes the political decisions in Fatah, but in a society as young as Palestine's, it is leaving its mark day in and day out. The only Israelis this generation knows are soldiers and settlers. For this generation, Israel is no more than a subsidiary of an army that knows no limits and settlements that know no borders.

---

1. Hebrew for "Gentiles."

2. Israeli town north of Tel Aviv, population: 70,000.

April 19, 2002

Leaning on a cane, the man stood on a mountain of ruins: a jumble of crushed concrete, twisted iron rods, mattress shreds, electric cables, fragments of ceramic tiles, pieces of water pipes, and an orphaned light switch. "This is my home," he said, "and my son is inside." His name is Abu Rashid. His son, Jamal, 35, was confined to a wheelchair. The bulldozer began to gnaw at the house while the family was still inside. And where would they be, if not in the house, seeking—like all the residents of Jenin Refugee Camp—the safest place to hide from the mortar and rocket and machine gun fire, praying for a brief respite? Abu Rashid and the other family members hurried to the front door, went out with their hands up, and tried to yell to the huge bulldozer, the operator of which was unseen and unheard, that there were people inside. But the bulldozer did not stop roaring, retreating and then attacking again, returning and taking another bite out of the concrete wall, until it collapsed on Jamal before anyone could save him.

All around Abu Rashid people were climbing up or down heaps of debris, making their way between piles of cement, sharp iron rods, metal fragments, concrete pillars, collapsed ceilings, and sections of sinks. Not all of them were as introverted as Abu Rashid, who talked to himself more than to the people who had stopped to listen to him. There were those who tried to rescue something from the ruins: a garment, a shoe, a bag of rice. Nearby, a young girl, who almost fell on a pile of broken cement blocks, pointed to the ceiling at her feet, and just cried. Between sobs, she managed to say that this had been her parents' home and that she did not know who was buried beneath it, who managed to get away, whether anyone was alive under the ruins, who would get them out, or when.

Between the ruins, and amidst partially standing houses—the still-upright walls of which are riddled with bullet holes of all shapes and sizes—a broad expanse has been created. Where until two weeks ago several houses stood, some three stories high, IDF bulldozers went over the piles of cement several times, flattening them, grinding them to dust, "making a 'Trans-Israel highway'," as A put it. His home also fell victim to the bulldozers. Someone indicated a small opening in a pile of rubble from which cries for help could be heard until Sunday night. By Monday morning there were no more sounds coming from it. Someone else pointed to what had been a house where two sisters lived. Someone said that they are crippled. It is still not known whether they are buried under the rubble or got out of the camp in time.

There are houses that were empty when they were demolished. In some cases the soldiers ordered people to leave, so that they would not be killed. One old man, people said, refused to leave his home. "Fifty years ago you expelled me from Haifa. Now I have nowhere to go," he said. The soldiers lifted the stubborn old man and hauled him out. And there were cases in which they did not bother to issue a warning and the bulldozers moved in. Without prior announcement over a loudspeaker, without checking whether anyone was inside. That is what happened on Sunday, April 14th to the members of the Abu Bakr family, who live between the refugee camp and Jenin proper. On both the city and the camp, curfew had been imposed; soldiers were roaming the streets with tanks and armored vehicles, as well as on foot, shooting from time to time, tossing around stun grenades and blowing up suspicious objects. But compared to the previous week, it was quiet. There was no more helicopter fire, no more gun battles with a handful of armed Palestinian activists. But all of a sudden, at four in the afternoon, the Abu Bakr family heard the sound of a wall being crushed. The father of the family went outside, waved a white flag and yelled to the soldiers: "We are in the house! Where do you want us to go, why are you demolishing our home with us inside?" They yelled to him: "Go on, get inside," and stopped the bulldozer.

The narrow seam-line where the house is located has in recent days served as a bridge between the city and the camp. The residents of the city, many of whom come from the refugee camp, have tried to evade the soldiers and bring their relatives and friends some water, food, and cigarettes. At the Abu Bakr home they concluded that the soldiers wanted to widen the area that separates the city from the camp in order to prevent such "smuggling." In the evening, an armored vehicle was positioned next to the house and soldiers combed the surrounding yard. Then the armored vehicle left. M went to make coffee. He managed to put a teaspoon of sugar into the pot and began to stir the boiling water when someone or something came flying through the window, broke the glass, and set the kitchen on fire. A stun grenade? A tear-gas canister? Did the soldiers outside think someone was firing at them when he lit the gas burner? M thanks God that only his hands and face were burned by the flames—which were immediately extinguished—and that the other family members were not hurt, and that the house was not destroyed.

Muhammad al-Sba`a, 70, was not so lucky. On Monday, April 8th the bulldozers thundered near his home in the Hawashin neighborhood in the center of the camp. He went out of his house to tell the soldiers that there were people inside: he, his wife, their two sons, their son's wives, and seven children. He was shot in his doorway—hit in the head—related one of his sons this week. Members of his family managed to drag him inside. But then they were ordered to come out. The men were arrested, then released, and taken to the village of Rumani, northwest of Jenin. The women were taken to the Red Crescent building. The father remained in the house. When the men returned, there was no house. They can only hope that the father was killed on the spot and did not bleed to death, or die inside the ruins.

The destruction of dozens of homes by bulldozers began on Saturday, April 6th—four days after the IDF attack on Jenin began. It is still unknown how many people were buried beneath the rubble. The horrible smell of decaying bodies—and new ones are being discovered every day—mingles with the stench of uncollected garbage, burning garbage, and the surprising sent of geraniums, roses, and mint growing between the bougainvillea bushes that people have cultivated in the narrow strips of earth between their crowded houses. When the time comes, UNRWA[1] and the Red Cross will compile lists of the detained, the wounded, and the missing. But right now the most urgent task is the distribution of water, food, and medicines. The camp has been defined a disaster area.

Heavy shooting and shelling from tanks, beginning with the IDF attack on the night of Tuesday, April 2nd, preceded the demolition of houses. The tanks surrounded the camp, took up position on the hill to the west of it, and took over the main street. Two days later, the IDF began firing from helicopters: rocket and machine gun fire. People took shelter under staircases, on ground floors, in interior bathrooms, in storage rooms, in inner courtyards. People crowded into small rooms, holding each other in the dark, frightened. They covered their ears and shut their eyes, hugging the small, howling children.

When the shooting died down, they relate, they went out and found their houses in the following states: scorched—smoke and dust rising from them; riddled with holes; floors shaky; doors and windows ripped out; windowpanes smashed to bits; gaping holes in outer walls. The turn of damage statistics will also come, and when it does, UN teams will relay how many houses were destroyed by bulldozers; how many were damaged by shooting and whether they can be repaired or demolishing them is safer; how many families were in them; how many individuals. Um Yasser rescued a one-year-old baby from her neighbor's house, which was shelled. Rizq, the baby's father, she related, crawled out with both legs injured and his back severely burned. He came out bleeding with outstretched arms, she said. The house was surrounded by soldiers. Along came a military doctor or paramedic who cleaned and bandaged the wounds. Then soldiers took him to the cemetery and dumped him there. Neighbors who saw him gathered him and called a doctor. They finally managed to get him to a hospital a week after he was wounded.

H and her family were in their house when it was bombarded. They ran to take cover in her father's home nearby. H thinks that this was on April 8th. People find it hard to remember exact dates. The entire attack has become a jumble of fear and blood and destruction, without nights or days. Y's husband was shot when he stepped out the door. She dragged him to her father's house. There, they bandaged his leg, prayed that everything would be all right, and only managed to get him to a private hospital on Sunday, April 14th—evading the soldiers who patrolled the alleys on foot. A was wounded while performing an IDF mission: a foot patrol took him from his house and ordered him to walk ahead of them and open his neighbors' doors. A did as he was told, and as he stood by one of the doors, another unit appeared. Perhaps they thought he belonged to the *muqawamin* (resisters, armed activists), because no one else dared to roam the streets in the first days of the IDF invasion. He was shot and wounded. For four days he lay in the home of neighbors, until his brothers managed to get him treatment. Their house, located up the hill on the second floor of a multi-family building, was damaged by three to five rockets and countless bullets. Soldiers took over a nearby house, and just shot. His mother tells the story at length, leading visitors from one destroyed room to the next. And then she takes us out to the garden: he loved to plant things, he loved life, not death, she said of her son. Her other sons offered the visitors fruit from the garden: pleasantly tart loquats, refreshingly juicy plums. Most of the water tanks in the camp were punctured during the first days from the shooting, and the water pipes ruptured by IDF bulldozers and tanks. The supply of fresh water was cut off immediately. Therefore, when every drop counts, biting into these fruits is truly revitalizing.

Like many others, Abu Raed, 51, was also "enlisted" for IDF missions. For five days he accompanied the soldiers. During the day he walked ahead of them, from house to house, knocking on doors as soldiers concealed themselves behind him, aiming their rifles at the door and at him. At night, he was forced to stay with them in one of the houses they occupied. They hand-cuffed him and two soldiers guarded him, he said. At the end of his mission, they told him to stay in a certain house, alone. All around him the bulldozers and tanks roared. One of the tanks rolled onto the house. Abu Raed jumped to another house, leaping from one destroyed house to another until he reached his own home, which he also found partially destroyed—hit by three rockets. There were 13 people in the house when the rock-ets landed on it.

S said she was lucky. Her home was only occupied for a week, like a dozen other houses that climb the hillside. S is a widow who lives with her brother and his family in a house on the western edge of the camp: four adults, ten children. Most of the residents left the neighborhood before the IDF invaded. On the first and second nights, soldiers took over two or three houses adjacent to that of S and her family. The family took shelter in the kitchen, thinking it was the most protected room. Suddenly, in the middle of the night, someone came in through the wall, made a gaping hole near the floor and entered directly over 8-year-old Ribhiya's head. Windowpanes shattered and the room was covered in dust. The 14 people in the kitchen began to scream. Through the hole in the wall they heard someone shouting in Arabic: "Anyone who leaves the house will die." They peeked and saw a group of soldiers in the narrow alley. They tried to negotiate with the soldiers; perhaps they would go to the neighbors' house, to a safer room, but the only answer they heard was: "Whoever leaves the house will die."

After a while, the soldiers made a hole in the wall adjacent to the stairwell and came in through that. The family, huddled together in a corner, looked on in astonishment as more and more soldiers poured in, their faces painted black. The family was moved to another room, full of dust and broken glass. They were held there from the evening until early Friday morning. The soldiers, related S, did not allow them to leave the dimly lit room. When they pleaded to go to the bathroom, the soldiers brought them a pot from the kitchen. S's brother-in-law was arrested, and three women and their children were left alone in a house full of soldiers.

At dawn, S opened the door and discovered a different group of soldiers. With hand gestures and body language she signaled that she wanted to go to the bathroom, to take the children to the bathroom, to bring food. Someone who looked to her like an officer said to go ahead. She had to make her way on tiptoe through any number of soldiers lying on the floor of her home. The filth she found in the bathroom disgusted her. The officer standing beside her hung his head and she concluded that he was ashamed of what he saw. He went to a nearby house— where no one was home—brought water, and cleaned the bathroom. When they departed a week later the soldiers left behind a large pile of leftover food rations.

During the night, when the family was locked in one room, the soldiers searched the house. They emptied drawers and cupboards, overturned furniture, broke the television, cut the phone line, took away the telephone and broke a hole in another wall that leads to a neighboring apartment. Along the broken wall is a picture, painted in watercolors by her sister-in-law's brother, when he was 15 years old. A Swiss landscape: a lake, snowcapped mountains, evergreens, a deer, a house with a red-tiled roof and smoke curling from the chimney. By the shore of the lake he painted two mustached men dressed as Palestinians, riding a donkey. The date: May 10, 1996. The signature: Ashraf Abu al-Hayja.

Abu al-Hayja was killed by a rocket on one of the first days of the IDF attack. On Tuesday of last week his scorched body still lay in one of the rooms of a half-destroyed house. Abu al-Hayja was an activist with Hamas who, together with members of other armed groups, vowed to defend the camp to the death. Two of JZ's nephews were among the armed men who were killed, and he estimates that altogether they numbered no more than 70. "But everyone who helped them saw themselves as part of the resistance: those who signaled from afar that soldiers were approaching, those who hid them, those who made them tea," said JZ. According to him, no door in the camp was closed to them when they fled from the soldiers. The people of the camp, he said, decided not to abandon them, not to leave the fighters to their own devices. This was a collective decision, taken by each person individually.

Despite his connection to many of the armed men, JZ admits that it is hard for him to describe how the fighting transpired; how the resistance fighters and Israeli soldiers were killed. "From our reconstructions, it appears that the army attacked the camp with tank and machine gun fire from several directions at once, and tried to get their infantry in. But because of our fighters' resistance, they failed. Then they proceeded to attack all the houses in the camp indiscriminately, with helicopters and tanks. The soldiers who took over the houses at the edge of the camp signaled where not to fire and hit." Gradually, the armed Palestinians were pushed deeper into the camp, to their last battles.

JZ is a construction worker who built his own home, as well as those of many of his friends. His house was destroyed by several rockets. Currently, he sleeps at the home of his young friend, AM. When darkness descends on the camp—whose electricity has been cut off since April 3rd—candlelight radiates from only a few windows. There is a false confidence that a home from which no light emanates will not be hit. IDF fire continues intermittently, though there are no longer any Palestinians who will shoot back at the soldiers. From time to time, the silence is broken by the sound of an explosion. Anxiety and uncertainty are overcome momentarily in a discussion with AM's mother and aunt. On Monday evening the conversation with the Israeli guest began with the enumeration of those JZ knows to be dead: seven of them armed men killed in battle, and ten civilians—among them three women and at least two old men. There are scores of people whose fate is still unknown. The conversation jumps from memories of Ketziot,[2] where JZ was imprisoned during the first Intifada, to a soldier who, someone told AM, left his skullcap in a house he had searched. Heavy shooting enveloped the neighborhood, including the house where he left the skullcap. The soldier told a young Palestinian who had been "enlisted" that if he brought him the skullcap, he would be released. Dodging bullets, the young man ran into the house, brought out the skullcap, and was allowed to go home. JZ tells another story that is going around the camp, about soldiers who were attacked inside a house, which they fled, leaving their weapons behind. It is said that one of them cried: "Mother, mother, what kind of war is this?"

---

1. United Nations Relief and Works Agency for Palestine Refugees in the Near East.

2. Also known as 'Ansar 3'—a detention camp in the Negev set up by Israel during the first Intifada.

May 6, 2002

No one thought that the Palestinian Ministry of Culture, which takes up five of the eight stories of a brand new building in the center of al-Bireh, would be spared the fate of other Palestinian Authority (PA) offices in Ramallah and other cities—that is, the near total destruction of its contents and especially its high-tech equipment. After all, IDF troops were positioned in the building for about a month. Armored vehicles were parked in front and all around the familiar pictures of destruction accumulated: crushed cars, earth ramparts, deep ditches carved into the roads, broken sidewalks, stone fences shattered to bits, toppled electricity poles, loose cables, and clouds of dust and dirt enveloping every vehicle, tree, and roof in ever-thickening layers.

The Ministry of Culture is located in the large residential area that the IDF has kept under curfew even after its partial withdrawal from Ramallah on April 21st, when it shifted its focus to the siege on PA Chairman Yasser Arafat's headquarters. Every night the neighbors, who hid in their homes, could hear the sounds of objects being hurled out the windows of the Ministry of Culture and smashing on the ground below. In the ten days that preceded the lifting of the siege on Arafat's compound, the force in this building spent every night shooting at the Asra building, a large commercial center located just down the hill from the ministry. At first, the residents tried to locate armed Palestinians who might have opened fire in the direction of the post. But there were no armed Palestinians.

The neighbors concluded, therefore, that this was the soldiers' nightly entertainment. All they could do was lie awake for four or five hours each night and listen, against their will, to the incessant shooting at the windows and walls of the Asra building, which would cause pieces of stone facade to crash onto the roof of a small stone house next door with a thud that echoed throughout the valley. After a bullet struck the home of H, who lives with her two daughters, they decided to leave. One night the neighborhood awoke to the sound of dogs barking: they saw that someone had attached a loudspeaker to a tape player and was playing a recording of barking dogs. Within minutes all the dogs in the neighborhood joined the racket. Very soon, the barking reached more distant neighborhoods—another sleepless night.

This is an established neighborhood of single-story or two-story stone houses, surrounded by gardens with cypress and fruit trees. L remembers how her husband planted some of those trees several decades ago. The rural character of the neighborhood was unaffected by its proximity to the busy main streets and tall commercial buildings that have sprung up in the past decade. A few days after the partial withdrawal, residents were astonished to hear bulldozers mowing down the row of shade-giving cypresses. One cypress tree was placed across the road—a natural barrier against cars—and a fruit laden apricot tree was uprooted from the garden of a woman whose entire life revolves around her 35-year-old mentally handicapped son.

On the evening of Wednesday, May 1st when the siege on Arafat's compound was lifted and the armored vehicles and tanks rolled out, the ministry officials who rushed to the building did not expect to find it how they left it. Employees of the local radio and television station, Amwaj, also hurried to the scene, as did the employees of the local television station, Istiqlal, which together take up three of the building's floors. But what awaited them surpassed even their worst fears, and deeply shocked the representatives and cultural attachés of foreign consulates, who visited the site the following day. As in other offices, all the high-tech and electronic equipment was either ruined or missing—computers, photocopy machines, cameras, scanners, hard drives, editing equipment worth thousands of dollars, television monitors. The broadcast antenna atop the building was destroyed. Telephones vanished. A collection of Palestinian art objects (mostly hand embroideries) disappeared. Perhaps it was buried under heaps of documents and furniture; perhaps it was taken. Furniture was dragged from place to place, piled up, broken by soldiers. Gas heaters were overturned and thrown upon scattered papers and books, broken diskettes and discs, and smashed windowpanes.

In the Department for the Encouragement of Children's Art, the soldiers smeared the walls with gouache paints, destroying the children's paintings that hung there. In every room of the various departments—literature, film, children and youth culture—books, discs, pamphlets, and documents were amassed, and soiled with urine and excrement.

There are two toilets on every floor, but the soldiers urinated and defecated everywhere else, including in the rooms where they lived for a month. They did their business on the floors, in emptied-out flowerpots, even in desk drawers. They defecated into plastic bags, and these were scattered about. Some of them burst. Someone even managed to defecate into the photocopy machine.

The soldiers urinated into empty water bottles. These too were scattered by the dozen throughout the building, in cardboard boxes, among the piles of damaged goods, on desks, under desks, next to the furniture the soldiers smashed, among the children's books that they tossed around. Some of the bottles had opened and their yellow liquid contents spilled out, staining the thin wall-to-wall carpeting. It was especially difficult to enter two of the building's floors for the unbearable stench of feces and urine. Soiled toilet paper was also strewn everywhere.

In some rooms, not far from the mounds of feces and toilet paper, remains of rotting food were also scattered. In one corner, in the room where someone defecated into a drawer, cartons of fruits and vegetables had been left behind. The toilets were overflowing with urine-filled bottles, feces, and toilet paper.

Relative to other places, the soldiers did not leave behind much graffiti on the walls. Here and there was a Menorah, a Star of David, or praise for the Jerusalem soccer team Beitar. Someone forgot to take his dog tag with him. His name is recorded in the newspaper's editorial desk. Now the Palestinian Ministry of Culture is considering whether to leave the building as is. A memorial. At press time, the IDF spokesman had yet to respond.

May 19, 2002

According to representatives of donor countries and international organizations operating in the territories, the Israeli army has begun demanding that Palestinians obtain special permits from their local Civil Administration offices to move between one West Bank town or village and another. A senior Israeli security source has confirmed the new policy. According to the Palestinian Authority (PA), it is an institutionalization of Israel's policy of encirclement and cantonization. Israel's Coordinator of Operations in the Territories, Amos Gil`ad, says that the move aims to make things easier for the Palestinian population, as long as the policies of closure and encirclement continue. Contrary to peoples' fears, he said, it is not a political plan in the guise of a humanitarian gesture.

Under the new policy, goods will be transported from one Palestinian territory to another using the "back-to-back" system in which one truck unloads goods that are then loaded onto another truck in specially designated areas on the outskirts of the major towns. Pedestrians, as well as drivers, will be left with one entrance/exit into each area, which can be crossed only after obtaining the proper movement permit. These details were conveyed by Amos Gil`ad to representatives of the donor countries and international organizations working in the territories ten days ago.

Donor country representatives say that the new measure effectively divides the West Bank into eight isolated regions, with movement between them controlled by the IDF. The eight regions are Jenin, Nablus, Tul Karm, Qalqilya, Ramallah, Jericho, Bethlehem, and Hebron. Organizations such as the Red Cross employ a large number of Palestinians, and in a meeting with Israeli officials they were told to apply to the Civil Administration to request movement permits for their employees. They were told that the permits would be valid from 5:00am to 7:00pm and must be renewed monthly. A donor country representative said donor countries and international organizations were holding discussions to hammer out a unified response to this new measure. The source added that to date, the organizations have not submitted requests for permits. He noted that even if the measure was presented as temporary, there was much concern that the division of the territory into eight isolated regions would become permanent. Donor country representatives have briefed their governments about the changing situation and are awaiting a diplomatic response. They also reported the change to the Palestinian Authority, which had not been briefed by the Israelis.

Palestinians learned of the institutionalization of the encirclement policy in the past two weeks, following procedural changes at the Qalandia checkpoint[1] and the reinforcement of IDF troops deployed on the outskirts of other towns. Indeed, West Bank residents have been forbidden to cross the Qalandia checkpoint for a while now (only Palestinians in possession of Jerusalem ID cards and special humanitarian cases are permitted to pass). But it is only recently that soldiers at checkpoints have begun ordering them to go to the Civil Administration at Beit El to obtain a permit to leave Ramallah altogether. This particularly affects teachers who work in villages south and west of Ramallah. The Palestinian Ministry of Education has instructed teachers not to apply for movement permits.

Ophir Hacham, spokesman for the office of the Coordinator of Operations in the Territories, stated that, "arrangements for simple and proper documentation have been made to facilitate movement between the areas that are under encirclement. We would prefer, were it possible, to cancel the closures and encirclements, and with them the need for permits, but the closures and encirclements originate in the need to defend ourselves from the threat of murder through terror, and as long as the security situation is such and renders life difficult for the civilian population, the Coordinator of Operations in the Territories will continue to act to alleviate their hardships with the appropriate procedures."

------

1. South of Ramallah.

June 2, 2002

A`adli Nafa`a has three options for getting his mother, a recent amputee, to her follow-up treatment at the government hospital in Ramallah. He can call an ambulance from Ramallah. However, the ambulance, instead of traveling the seven kilometers from the city to Nafa`a's village of Dir Ibziya, will have to make a detour of about 60 kilometers on roads designated for Israelis only (and that too only after exhaustive, and exhausting, coordination with the army). The ambulance will also have to pass through the bottlenecked and tedious Qalandia checkpoint, and the long journey will cost Nafa`a 400 NIS, an astronomical sum for someone who has been unemployed for four months.

The second option is for him to take the same route he traveled on April 19th, when he took his diabetic mother to the hospital after the gangrene in her leg had worsened. He carried her on his back and walked through the hills, evading Israeli army posts, until he reached a village southwest of Dir Ibziya where he met up with an ambulance that had traveled eastward, on roads forbidden to Palestinian traffic. The soldier at the Qalandia checkpoint demanded that he get out of the ambulance and let the medical team transport his mother without him. Half an hour of pleading softened the soldier's heart and Nafa`a was permitted to accompany his mother, finally reaching the hospital at five in the afternoon. They had left home eight hours earlier, at nine in the morning.

The third option is to risk being shot at when approaching on foot—with his mother on his back—the system of trenches, earth ramparts, rocks, and barbed wire fencing, which the army has set up across the asphalt road east of the village. At the top of the hill, above the trenches and barricades, is an army post. The soldiers obey their orders to prevent any movement between the villages of Dir Ibziya and `Ayn Ariq, and shoot in the air to drive off violators. Thus, most of the day, the narrow stretch of road—the short and obvious route between Ramallah and some 25 villages to its west—is empty of both people and cars. People do take chances though: sometimes the armored personnel carrier (APC) stationed at the top of the hill goes on patrol, and they slip past the barbed wire and ramparts and run to catch a group taxi concealed among the houses on the edge of `Ayn Ariq. This is how Nafa`a brought his mother back home on May 8th, after spending two weeks at her bedside.

On the evening of February 19, 2002, Palestinians killed six soldiers stationed at the `Ayn Ariq-Dir Ibziya checkpoint. Since then, over three months later, all traffic is barred from this, the only road to Ramallah still available to the tens of thousands of residents of the area's two-dozen villages. The nearby highways that serve Jewish settlements are also off limits to Palestinian vehicles, and the paths connecting the villages to each other are blocked by earth ramparts, making travel impossible. As a result, thousands of people have difficulty reaching their places of work and sources of income.

For three months now the regular supply of food and medicine has been severely disrupted. Aside from the fact that people have lost their livelihoods, with the little money at their disposal they cannot find food in the stores, certainly not fresh food. Soldiers frequently prevent villagers from reaching their own orchards on the outskirts of villages. The doctor who used to come out from Ramallah each day has stopped coming. He had enough when soldiers shot at him from the hilltop as he tried to cross the ramparts to get to the village of Na`ama. In the clinic at Dir Ibziya there is a nurse who dispenses medication without a doctor's prescription. Babies are not vaccinated on time. Pregnant women leave for Ramallah, through the hills, two weeks before their due date. Patients do not go for routine checkups, and miss regular treatments, like dialysis. Teachers who live outside the village sometimes reach their schools, and sometimes don't.

After exhaustive coordination with the Civil Administration, food shipments were allowed into Dir Ibziya twice via the Red Cross. The trucks were forced to take a long and circuitous route. On March 27, 2002 the organization delivered several hundred kilograms of food provided by the Palestinian Ministry of Supply. The second shipment, in early May, was donated by Caritas, a Christian organization. (Despite prior agreement, the soldiers refused to allow its transfer from one truck to another over the ramparts and trenches). In the village, the food was received with mixed feelings. "They are forcing us to become welfare recipients," grumbled a professor of hydrology at Bir

Zeit University, who insists on climbing the hills each day in order to get to work.

The `Ayn `Ariq checkpoint was erected in the Spring of 2001. Soldiers supervised the movement of thousands of people who passed through it daily, delaying them for hours at a time—especially in the early morning when they were rushing to work and in the late afternoon when they were in a hurry to get home. The writer was witness to these delays on more than one occasion and frequently alerted the IDF spokesman to this and other complaints. For example, that soldiers often throw tear gas and stun grenades at the hassled and exhausted people. A young Palestinian was killed by the IDF in late January. He had a shoving match with a soldier and another soldier shot him, claiming that he had tried to draw a knife from the soldier's flack-jacket. The young man was wounded in the leg and dragged to the soldiers' post. Army sources claim that the Palestinian medical team that treated him was not sufficiently trained or equipped. Palestinian sources say that the treatment for staunching blood is simple and if it had been administered in time the incident would not have resulted in death.

Some three weeks later, six soldiers were killed. That same night, the checkpoint was dismantled. The next morning, the asphalt was torn up, earth ramparts were laid down, and barbed wire fencing was erected. A blanket curfew was placed on all the surrounding villages, especially Dir Ibziya. After a few days, people began to venture out. Little by little they came, at first just to the village center, then to its outskirts. However, say the villagers, the few shops that tried to open were hit with tear gas. The soldiers also made it clear that it was forbidden to drive around in the village. During the first month they would shoot at the tires of "disobedient" vehicles or slash them, including the spares. Some soldiers poured sand into gas tanks, and others confiscated car keys, returning them two days later.

The IDF spokesman confirms that movement between Dir Ibziya and `Ayn `Ariq is forbidden to Palestinians, "with the exception of humanitarian and medical cases, or those that have been coordinated in advance." It seems that the area commanders did not inform the IDF spokesman that soldiers also forbid cars to move within the village itself and sometimes prevent the movement of pedestrians too (the writer witnessed such an incident on May 24, 2002). The IDF spokesman states: "The movement of pedestrians and vehicles is permitted within the boundaries of every village," and is not aware of complaints regarding slashed tires, sand in gas tanks, or confiscated car keys. "This is very serious behavior and disciplinary measures will be taken against offenders if the complaints are made explicit and found to be correct."

But people have to get to work and medical treatments, and students have to get to their classes at Bir Zeit University or the al-Quds Open University. All of them sneak through the hills. The game of cat and mouse that developed between soldiers and local residents on March 27th was clear: taxis approached the gas station as soon as the APCs and jeeps were out of sight. Passengers got out quickly and advanced on foot towards the hills, through the olive groves.

Suddenly an APC appeared at the gas station, unloading soldiers who reprimanded the one driver who had not managed to get away: "You know you are not supposed to be driving around." According to the gas station attendants, were it not for the presence of the writer, the soldiers would have been less polite. In the distance a car was spotted. "Let's go get him," said one soldier to another and they took off. A taxi appeared from nowhere and took advantage of the presence of journalists to fill his tank (soldiers have prohibited the station owner from replenishing his supply of gasoline. The IDF spokesman knows nothing of this).

A woman of about 60 approached the gas station, out of breath. She came from Ramallah. She rode as far as `Ayn Ariq, and from there began to climb through the hills. With soldiers roaming the streets of Dir Ibziya, there was no chance she would find a taxi that would risk driving her to her village of Na`ama. She was forced to continue climbing on foot. But first, she sat on the chair offered her by the gas station attendants and wiped away her sweat. It was a rainy day.

Every day soldiers catch people climbing through the hills and return them to their starting point. People carry bags with a little bread, a few vegetables, and some dairy products—light things so that they can still run from the soldiers. On Wednesday, May 22nd a group of 90 people—men, women, and children—were detained in the hills from three in the afternoon until ten at night. Kamal al-Tawil, a resident of Dir Ibziya, told the writer that the soldiers brought the people down from the hills near the trenches, where they were made to kneel with bowed heads. After seven hours they were forced to return to Ramallah in the dark, though their homes were in the nearby villages. On May 23rd soldiers turned back all the people caught in the hills disobeying orders, apart from one woman who managed to convince them that she was bringing her son back from the hospital. This too, after being detained for two hours.

That same day, 30-year-old `Aliyah Sadqa, from the village of Na`ama, was injured in her leg by IDF gunfire. She and her two-year old son got out of a taxi at the foot of the road leading to `Ayn `Ariq. She hadn't intended to cross the trenches but to climb the hill and walk along its winding paths in order to bypass the soldiers. But the soldiers have picked up on the local residents' "tricks," and spot the taxis as they drop off passengers intending to climb by foot. They shoot at them while they are still on the incline. Sadqa was wounded in the thigh, near her groin. She fell to the ground as her young son looked on in horror.

The soldiers hurried away and local residents called an ambulance. Sadqa does not know how long she lay there; she just remembers reciting passages from the Quran. Her injury turned out not to be critical and she was brought home by ambulance some ten days later. Sadqa's relatives who came to collect her knew that an Israeli journalist was present in the village and asked the latter to accompany them through the trenches and barbed wire, and from there to Na`ama, so that the soldiers would not prevent her from returning home.

The IDF spokesman says that the incident is "not known," but that following the writer's query, it will be investigated and disciplinary action will be taken "if the troops did not act in accordance with procedure." The spokesman did not answer the question whether someone from Dir Ibziya or the surrounding villages has been arrested on suspicion of killing the six soldiers. Nor did he explain how Nafa`a was supposed to transport his mother to the hospital. The IDF spokesman also failed to respond to the local residents' complaint that they are being subjected to revenge in the form of collective punishment. On March 27, 2002, soldiers told the writer: "Were it revenge we would blow the whole village up."

June 26, 2002

A radio interviewer asked IDF Spokesman Ron Kitrey on Sunday about the three children killed in Jenin by Israeli soldiers in a tank (which also killed a 60-year-old man). The interviewer chose his words carefully. So carefully, that he asked Kitrey about the "youths" who were killed. These "youths" were 6-year-old Soujoud Turkey, 6-year-old Ahmed Ghazawi, and his 12-year-old brother Jamil. The two brothers had been riding their bicycles in the neighborhood. They, like many others, thought that the curfew had been lifted for several hours. Soujoud Turkey had gone with her father to buy some bread.

The interviewer stammered slightly as he posed his question, perhaps because in these days of suicide bombings it is not considered polite to discuss Palestinian casualties. Turning them into "youths" was not a slip of the tongue. It reflects a phenomenon. Even before suicide attacks became routine, the IDF's civilian victims simply evaporated, and continue to evaporate, for Israeli society. They are perceived as politically and militarily irrelevant.

This is not about appealing to one's sense of morality and compassion, nor is it about ignoring Israeli pain. It is about being able to analyze why the conflict has turned into a bloody cycle of violence spun out of control. Analyze, so as to gain control over it. Most Israelis' analytical ability is impaired by their collective political consciousness and unwillingness to take the cumulative Palestinian pain from this Intifada, and the Oslo years that preceded it, into account.

Israeli political consciousness has refused, and continues to refuse, to grasp the sum total of the details, characteristics, actions, and consequences of ongoing Israeli rule over another people. When one tries to talk of the "totality" known as the occupation, the media—our social barometer—respond with resentment. This "totality" is too abstract, transparent, and academic. Let's talk about "human interest" stories instead. But when one talks about personal experiences that is exactly how they are perceived: another tearjerker about a suffering Palestinian individual. Before the Intifada, such stories (deaths at roadblocks, Israeli quotas on drinking water, bans on building schools in Area C, settlement expansion, restrictions on the freedom of movement) were understood as anomalies in the "peace process," though they affected Palestinians day in and day out.

Today, reports on "Palestinian suffering" are perceived as national treason. Israelis conclude that the suicide bombings are the result of a murderous tendency inherent to the Palestinians, their religion, and their mentality. In other words, people turn to bio-religious explanations, not socio-historical ones. This is a grave mistake. If one wants to put an end to the terror attacks in general, and the suicide bombings in particular, one must ask why the majority of Palestinians support them. Without their support, the Palestinian organizations would not dare to dispatch suicide bombers and "invite" the anticipated escalatory Israeli response. The Palestinians support the attacks, even the most ruthless ones, because they are convinced that they, their existence, and their future as a nation are the real targets of the Israeli regime—both when it applied rule-by-deceit tactics in the Oslo period, and now when it uses the tactics of military escalation and siege.

Israeli society did not heed Palestinian warnings during the Oslo years that an imposed agreement would lead to disaster. Nor did the Israeli political consciousness get it when, at the beginning of the Intifada, Palestinians pointed to Israel's excessive use of force against the first demonstrators. Now, 22 months later, one can find a few Israeli journalists and politicians who in hindsight admit that under Ehud Barak and Shaul Mofaz[1], excessive use was made of lethal force. If indeed there was any desire to control the frenzy of violence, the harsh military response was a mistake. But this excessive use of force has not been erased from the Palestinians' consciousness. And why should they forget their children who were killed just because they threw stones at armored jeeps, tanks and fortified outposts? Why should they forget the civilians killed by IDF fire at roadblocks and in their own homes, not during gun battles?

Now the Palestinians are driven by the same misguided notion that directed Barak, Mofaz, and the commanders on the ground at the outset of the Intifada, which Israeli society supported: more force and more killing and suffering, as quickly as possible, will teach the other side a lesson and foil their plans. The suicide bombings in Israel indicate impaired analytical ability on the part of most Palestinians. They fail to grasp that just as the daily killings by IDF soldiers and unbearable living conditions under the ever-tightening siege strengthen them, the Israeli response to the death sown in their midst by Palestinians is much the same. Both sides are convinced that only more deadly and devastating force will restrain the opposing side. Both sides are dead wrong.

––––––

1. IDF Chief of Staff under Ehud Barak and later Ariel Sharon.

June 27, 2002

Unemployed workers in Khan Yunis are demanding that the fruit stands be removed from the center of town. "The children ask why it has been so long since we bought them fruit—peaches, plums, apricots—everything that comes from Israel and costs 5, 6, 7 NIS per kilo," explains F with tears in his eyes. "They don't have anywhere to go during the summer vacation. The beach is closed to Palestinians, the road to Gaza is blocked more often than not, it is too dangerous to travel to the orchards and fields east of Khan Yunis because soldiers shoot from the border. So they roam the streets and see the piles of red and orange and yellow and ask if they are entitled to some fruit. As a father, I'm so ashamed." Whether they will succeed in getting the fruit stands removed remains to be seen. Some unemployed parents boast that they already managed to get the watermelon sellers off their streets.

The circle of unemployed workers swells from 10 to 20 to 30 as each tries to outdo the other in explaining how unbearable the situation has become. One man searches his pockets until he finds a half-shekel coin and an expired permit to work in Israel, which he saves like a treasured memento. Another man says his Israeli boss owes him two months' wages and is exploiting the closure to avoid paying him. A third man says that he got his last salary via the bank but when he asked if he was entitled to severance pay after three years' work, his employer told him: "I didn't fire you, it's not my responsibility." Another tells how his employer in Bat Yam[1] does send him a little money to tide him over until he can come back to work. "We've sold everything in the house, we've got nothing left," someone else says. "We're leaving our wives because we can't provide for them," says yet another, and the rest nod in agreement. "Last night my child cried of hunger until he fell asleep," someone admits, and everyone falls silent. Suddenly someone bursts out, "At the beginning of the Intifada the Arab states promised to send the workers money. Some of us received a grant once or twice: 500 NIS, another time 600 NIS. That's it. I received 600 NIS. According to my calculations, I got a shekel a day. We want to know where all the money is going."

The unemployed workers, most of whom had jobs in Israel until the Intifada broke out, are starting to make their voices heard. About five weeks ago, workers in northern Gaza set up protest tents on the main road leading into the Strip from the Erez crossing: one at the entrance to Beit Hanoun,[2] another on the road to the Jabalya Refugee Camp and a third inside Jabalya. "Why don't you protest in Gaza City, near the government offices? After all, almost no one passes by here," they were asked. The answer couldn't be simpler: they don't have the four shekels for the round trip ride to Gaza every day. Several members of the Palestinian Legislative Council (PLC) visited them, made declarations, expressed support, and left. The workers came up with the initiative of protest tents, and then contacted activists in Palestinian NGOs such as the Democracy and Workers' Rights Center, and PINGO—the umbrella organization for Palestinian NGOs dealing with human rights, women's empowerment, and health and agricultural advancement projects. Gradually, more protest tents sprung up—in the Shati Refugee Camp, in Khan Yunis, and in the Nuseirat Refugee Camp.

A demonstration is planned for July 1st and this time the organizers hope that unemployed workers from southern Gaza will join them in marching to Arafat's seaside bureau. Local workers' committees have formed as well as a central coordinating committee. A banner, signed "The Workers' Protest Tents—Gaza Strip," has been printed with the help of one of the NGOs. It features four desperate looking men holding various work implements: a shovel, a hoe, a pitchfork, pliers, and a trowel, foregrounding a crowded refugee camp filled with people raising their hands in a gesture implying: "What will be?" The banner states: "We want work and wages. We don't want handouts."

In the various protest tents, as well as outside the Palestinian Legislative Council (PLC) building in Gaza, the protesters pounce on the willing listener who has happened their way. They analyze their situation, argue among themselves, demand that the conversation be held in Arabic and not Hebrew—so everyone can understand, express nostalgia for the past and fear for the future. One person tells this story: "The Prophet Muhammad, peace be upon him, once saw a poor man sitting on a street corner. He asked who the man was and was told 'He's a Jew, an infidel.' The Prophet said: 'He used to work for you. Take him and attend to his needs.'" Others called out in response: "We built Israel. Who built Sharon's ranch? We built it!" Since 1967, Israel's economic policy in the territories, and especially in Gaza, was based on two principles: bringing cheap Palestinian labor into Israel and obstructing the development of an independent economy in the territories (by imposing restrictive laws and refusing to develop infrastructure, despite the fact that Palestinians paid taxes). Thus, the families of those working in Israel achieved relative economic prosperity on a personal level, while the community as a whole stayed economically backward. In Israel of the 1970s, the thinking was that economic dependence would avert separation and personal economic welfare would inhibit nationalist ideas about political independence. Even in the optimistic days of Oslo, economists explained that this dependence was still intact and that even if development plans went ahead unhindered, it would take years to create enough new jobs. Thus, economic stability in the territories—and especially in Gaza—depended on work in Israel. No one considered the possibility that this source of income would disappear.

Whenever someone in the crowd tries to point a blaming finger at the Palestinian Authority (PA), there is always someone who tries to shut him up. "The Jewish journalist is only interested in criticism of the PA," someone says with concern. But then the opposite view gains strength, especially outside the PLC. "I'm not afraid, let them arrest me," says one person, "I'll tell the truth." Last Wednesday, several Palestinian legislators looked out at the demonstrators from a high-up balcony and spoke words of encouragement. Rather conspicuously, photographers were there to capture the moment. The workers looked on from below and began losing patience. They silenced the speakers by shouting and banging on pots. "Everyone talks, everyone fakes, we don't believe them," the workers explained. "Write, write," they urge, "Why doesn't the Palestinian television come to our tent? Why doesn't the Palestinian press write about us?"

On the other hand, representatives of the Palestinian General Federation of Trade Unions were conspicuously absent. The Fatah members among them receive their salaries from the PA.

These officials distributed what was called the "Arafat Grant" to unemployed workers at the beginning of the Intifada. But there were accusations that some of these grants were passed along to senior labor officials' associates—people who were not even out of work. While difficult to prove, these charges reflect the distrust for people in leadership positions. Disappointment was also in store, of course, for anyone who thought that the Arab states would continue to pay monthly unemployment benefits to approximately 100,000 workers in the West Bank and Gaza who had been registered as workers in Israel. Workers are still asking, "Where is the money going?" and suspect that it is going into the pockets of senior officials. But the monthly donations of Arab (and European) governments cover about 65% of the PA's operating budget and non-governmental contributions are transferred to a network of charitable organizations supervised by the Palestinian Ministry of Interior. This month, the PA has yet to pay the salaries of 125,000 public sector employees (both civil servants and security personnel) because the donations earmarked for this expense have not arrived. Many of these public sector employees needed food packages this month, just like the unemployed workers.

The poverty and despair of the unemployed workers exacerbates their suspicion, engendering exaggerated accusations: "When the wages of the civil servants are two weeks late, they raise hell," one unemployed worker says. "But we have been living without salaries for 22 months." After a senior official appears before them in an attempt to convince them that "There is no money," the workers ask, "So how was he able to buy a plot of land just now?" or "He sends his children to study abroad, while I can't even send my son—who finished high school with excellent marks—to the al-Quds Open University," or "He feeds his dog two chickens a day, and I don't remember the last time I was able to feed my children poultry."

When the Palestinian workers who labored in Israel speak of the PA "neglecting their case," they know what they are talking about. Since the early 1970s, the Israeli authorities have deducted social security payments from the Palestinians' paychecks at the same rate as Israeli workers. But individual Palestinians have received only a small portion of these benefits (sick pay and worker's compensation). They never received unemployment benefits. When challenged in court, the state claimed that social security payments collected from Palestinians were collectively used for the development of the territories (during Israel's period of direct rule), but had difficulty documenting this allocation and development. In the framework of the negotiations, it was decided in 1994 that the social security payments collected from Palestinians in the past, together with those to be collected in the future, would be transferred to a special PA fund dedicated to the welfare of Palestinians employed in Israel.

But the PA never created this fund and has failed to provide a clear explanation for its neglect to do so. Thus, the money Palestinian workers continued to pay to the Sate of Israel for social security benefits was never passed on to the PA. If before the Intifada there was need to worry about the fate of these monies, today it is safe to assume that they will surely be swallowed up by the Israeli treasury along with all the other taxes and fees the government of Israel is obliged to transfer to the PA but has frozen. Due to the PA's negligence, the workers' representatives are demanding that the PA "not give handouts" but see to it that they get work or unemployment benefits until the situation improves and "the road [to Israel] reopens."

The subversive potential of the workers' protests has not eluded PA officials. They have already begun accusing the workers of opposing the PA instead of the Israeli occupation; of being pawns in the hands of oppositional [leftist] forces; of usurping, via the Palestinian NGOs, European donations that ought to benefit the masses. Unemployed workers say that the authorities have sent "spies" to their tents and that some of the activists have been promised jobs. Members of local committees have warned their fellow protestors of "provocateurs" and cautioned that protest activities remain non-violent. PA security personnel have taken down one tent in the Shati Refugee Camp and demanded that a landowner in Nuseirat dismantle a protest tent erected on his property.

The unemployed workers have hung their hopes on the new Minister of Finance, Salaam Fiad (currently under curfew in Ramallah), a Tul Karm native who previously represented the International Monetary Fund in the territories and is regarded as "an American appointee."

They expect him to tell them whether monies designated for them indeed disappeared and to act to re-divide the PA budget more equitably and transparently. Some of the workers insist that the Americans are interested in returning Palestinian workers to Israel "because they understand how dangerous poverty is to stability."

"On Gaza's borders, young people are killed by IDF fire. It is said they were on their way to carry out terror attacks, when they were really on their way to find work," one man says. A resident of Jabalya, whose family came from the village of Hoj (today Kibbutz Dorot), adds: "I don't want my land back. Land belongs to God. I want to work and live." A third man joins in: "Doesn't Israel understand how dangerous poverty is to everyone? Does Israel think it can just get rid of us? This situation makes everyone want to explode. I'm convinced that everyone who blew himself up had an unemployed brother."

---

1. Israeli town south of Tel Aviv, population: 140,000.

2. Palestinian village in the northern Gaza Strip, population: 20,000.

August 14, 2002

Some 700 Palestinian demonstrators waited in vain on Saturday evening for activists from Ta`ayush, a Jewish-Arab coexistence group, to arrive in Bethlehem for a joint demonstration in the occupied city. When it turned out that the IDF would not allow the two sides to meet, they decided to use mobile phones and loudspeakers to declare that "there is someone to talk to" on both sides. There were Palestinians who found it hard to believe the Israeli authorities would indeed prevent a peace demonstration from taking place. Someone said that he heard some young people hissing: "If they don't want peace demonstrations, they'll get attacks." Simplistic, but it says something about the working conditions for Palestinian groups and individuals who believe that terror attacks are wrong—strategically and morally—and that the militarization of the uprising from the outset may have been a mistake.

These people and groups are in a bind: they agree with the popular sentiment that Israeli rule in the territories is like a daily, even hourly, attack on three million Palestinians, which makes it difficult for them to disseminate their rational critique of suicide bombings (and the public support they engender) and argue that revenge is not a good rationale for conducting an uprising.

From the outset, the Palestinian leadership failed to come up with a clear strategy for carrying out the struggle. Israel, of course, is convinced that the Palestinian Authority (PA) initiated and orchestrated the whole thing. In the territories, however, people know that the PA was dragged into it. Yasser Arafat's solo decision-making style, coupled with senior PA officials' efforts to survive politically, and the fear that the uprising will turn against the PA itself, created a vacuum in Palestinian policy. This vacuum has been filled by military initiatives.

From the Palestinian public's perspective, attacks on Israel testify to the Palestinian organizations' incompetence and inability to conduct a classic guerrilla campaign in the territories like that waged by Hizballah in Lebanon. According to many in this public, efforts should be made to pinpoint the weak links in Israel's military deployment in the territories, rather than continuing to slip back and forth across the green line. Moreover, in the Palestinians' view, lethal escalation and popular support for it stem from their leadership's failure not only to achieve independence through negotiations, but also to use political and diplomatic means to stop the IDF's military assault.

Since the establishment of the PLO, the Palestinian national movement has sanctified the principle of armed struggle, sometimes to the point where it became the ends rather than the means. From there, it's a short leap to sanctifying anyone with a weapon, even if that "weapon" is a human being.

The admission of military and political weakness paved the way for escalation and a phenomenon that should be worrying every Palestinian: mass readiness on the part of young people to kill themselves so as to kill others. From the point of view of the lone suicide bomber, there is no real difference between the Islamic movements and the Fatah or other secular groups. The number of youths prepared to die is far greater than the number of attacks it is possible to plan. The Islamic movements have a clear interest in linking the phenomenon to Muslim precepts. Perhaps there has been an increase in the numbers of people who believe in eternal paradise. But secular Palestinian observers are sure that first comes the readiness to die, and only after that is religious faith applied.

Both religious and secular Palestinians are convinced that those prepared for self-sacrifice are acting within a political-military context in which Israel has overwhelming superiority and almost total control over Palestinian lives. Those who choose to die (in order to kill) are not necessarily frustrated on a personal level. They see themselves—and are perceived—as representing a collective frustration and fury over a life unworthy of the name, which the Palestinians believe to be the result of deliberate Israeli policy: lives in cages, poverty, and disease, accompanied by daily killings, prohibitions on movement, and humiliation. "If we are dead while alive, at least we can choose the time and manner of our revenge." This is a common sentiment expressed by Palestinians.

Meanwhile, the more Israel steps up its military campaign, the more the weakened Palestinian population's support for terror attacks, and suicide bombings in particular, grows. Rhetoric about ruthlessness does not convince them. They claim they have the right as individuals to respond ruthlessly to Israeli ruthlessness.

Suicide bombings by Fatah members are local, even personal, initiatives stemming from competition with Hamas over organizational popularity. For Hamas, it is a centralized, conscious strategy, not unrelated to internal struggles over the future Palestinian regime. As long as Hamas senses public support for the attacks, it will not give them up.

Beneath the surface there are many efforts to open public debate aimed at reducing Palestinian support for attacks inside Israel, without waiting for Israeli policy to change. The joint demonstration with Ta`ayush was just such an effort; an effort that failed thanks to the Israeli authorities.

September 4, 2002

In 1869, the first carriage road was paved between Jaffa and Jerusalem. Aside from it, narrow dirt paths connected cities and villages, and people traveled from place to place and transported goods mainly on foot or on donkeys, camels, or mules. An economy based for the most part on primitive agriculture and scant education fits in with this Palestinian road map, traced by historian Benny Morris in his book *Righteous Victims: a History of the Zionist-Arab Conflict, 1881-1999*. One can assume that the sense of common origin and destiny between these remote communities was still rather weak.

The level of connection between West Bank cities and villages today is fast approaching that of 150 years ago: people walk by foot on dirt paths or ride donkeys and tractors (the modern alternative to the camel) in order to fulfill basic needs like obtaining water, a few vegetables, medicines, and attending school. Distances are also starting to grow, and resemble those of the 19th century. It takes a few days to get from Ramallah to Jenin, and half a day to reach Hebron from Bethlehem. Haifa and Jaffa (and the relatives and friends who live there) have been wiped off the map for all practical purposes, though their beauty and significance in the Palestinian consciousness have reached legendary proportions.

If 150 years ago people had to be wary of thieves and bandits along the way, those walking through the hills and valleys today have to watch for army patrols and surprise roadblocks where a tank, an armored personnel carrier, or a police jeep might be stationed. They risk having citations written against them for violating the military order of internal closure banning travel without first obtaining a permit from the Civil Administration. Two million lawbreakers live in the West Bank, and an enormous army of law enforcers try to track down every breach in the fence, every roadblock cleared overnight, every dirt rampart flattened, and every new footpath carved out by anonymous footsteps.

These enforcers of law and order, using the most advanced means of surveillance, observe the "lower" Palestine of pedestrians and donkey-riders from the "upper" Land of Israel of spacious modern highways that serve a trickle of Israeli cars.

Internal closure, that is, the anti-modern process of reverting to

ancient transportation methods, is coupled with a modern muta-
tion of house arrest—to which half a million people have been
subject for over two months. The school year began on Saturday
and, except in Jenin and the Old City of Hebron, the curfew was
lifted in the cities during the day so that students could attend
school (and they were excited to do so!) after being locked up at
home for the entire summer vacation. But the curfew was re-
imposed on most of the cities on Sunday and Monday, and the
disappointed children were again jailed behind apartment walls.
Internal closure and prolonged house arrest have not only
reduced horizons to nothing (and made distances astronomical),
they have pushed the economy back, together with the level of
sanitation and health. The level of education is also declining,
despite official Palestinian denials and boasts of student achieve-
ment in recent matriculation exams. Since most of the population is now urban, it lacks the land reserves that provide villagers
with basic foodstuffs. In any case, even those who can grow a few
tomatoes and some squash in their villages, cannot readily access
their olive groves or sell their produce in the cities, as the markets
are closed due to the curfew. An entire population is therefore
forced into the status of dependents. The world finances the
unemployment benefits of about 120,000 public sector workers
and those registered as members of the Palestinian security apparatus; UNRWA distributes food to hundreds of thousands of
needy people with international funding; and Arab and Islamic
funds cover the distribution of food through private charities and
the Palestinian Authority.

Whether knowingly or not, whether intentionally or not, the
policies of internal closure and ongoing curfew are hurting—
even destroying—the modern national ties the Palestinian public
has developed over the past 100 years; shredding a collective into
a collection of individuals forced to deal, mostly on their own,
with an unbearable reality. This disintegration is consistent with

the 1970s Israeli outlook, which is coming back into fashion today: the Palestinians are not a "people" and are not entitled to the communal rights of a people in this land, but only to the rights of "individuals"—and that too is contingent upon their "good behavior." This disintegration is also consistent with the vision of disconnected enclaves proposed by Member of Knesset and former Minister of National Infrastructure, Avigdor Lieberman, and matches the so-called "interim solution" proposals being concocted by other Israeli groups.

Do people in Israel think that the Palestinian national consciousness can also be turned back to 1869, in order to make things easier for those who are cooking up interim solutions for what appears to be an interminable period of time?

November 13, 2002

Over a period of five days, K was "caught" wiping away tears three times. The first time he was speaking of his eldest son, whom he had sent to study abroad to distance him from any possible involvement in "futile efforts," as K put it, against the Israeli occupation such as throwing Molotov cocktails at tanks or blowing up, like one of his friends did, while planting a homemade charge along a torn-up road. The second time tears welled up in his eyes he was speaking of his factory, closed-down and wedged between the piles of dirt and rock that block the road and Tul Karm's northern gate, which, like the southern gate, is locked, turning the city into an isolated enclave, cut off from other West Bank enclaves and the rest of the world. The third time was when K encountered a short, gaunt man, entering the Palestinian welfare offices, and looking humiliated.

The man was the father of Omar Subuh, a member of the Abu Ali Brigades—named for Abu Ali Mustafa, the General Secretary of the Popular Front for the Liberation of Palestine (PFLP) assassinated by Israel in August 2001. About three weeks after Mustafa's assassination, just after the PFLP's military wing adopted the name "Abu Ali Brigades," Omar, the man's son, was riding in a car alongside a car carrying Raed Karmi, the head of Tul Karm's al-Aqsa Martyrs Brigades. A missile intended for Karmi hit Omar Subuh's car. He may have been on Israel's wanted list, but he was too unimportant to be targeted by a missile. Two of Omar's brothers have been arrested and a third is wanted. K introduced himself to the father and expressed his condolences. "My eldest son," he told him, "used to play with your son." He had difficulty looking at Abu Omar's gray face, which told the whole story: bereavement, longing, anxiety for the other sons, dire straits. K could not hold back his tears.

After regaining composure, K, a former PFLP activist, said that there is really no difference between the Abu Ali Brigades and the al-Aqsa Martyrs Brigades. "They are both military wings that don't change anything—semi-illiterate children pushed into playing heroes and fighters and leaders." Many, especially K's contemporaries, who were already adults during the first Intifada, share this unflattering view, but are careful to keep it to themselves. Do the armed groups terrorize the people, forcing them to keep their criticism under wraps?

One morning last month, it was difficult to see any "terror" on the faces of the people who hosted the Brigade members for the purpose of this interview. They showed no signs of fear or concern for the risk they were taking by having them in their homes. About two-dozen members of the al-Aqsa Martyrs Brigades live in Tul Karm, which the IDF controls from within and without. They live underground, sleeping in other people's homes. In some neighborhoods and refugee camps, people willingly endanger their lives to host them, and see this as natural, something to be taken for granted.

Four Brigade members, aged 21 to 26, all wanted by Israel, took part in the conversation. The oldest was 11 years old when the first Intifada began. His strongest memory of that time is the complete disruption of his studies. After the Palestinian Authority (PA) was formed, no attempt was made to compensate all those children for the lost years of schooling. Instead, they were recruited, especially the Fatah supporters among them, into the PA security apparatus or thrown into the Israeli labor market or put on West Bank unemployment rosters. Like the entire generation of the first Intifada, they grew up in the shadow of that uprising's repression: extended curfews, daily deaths, arrests that emptied entire neighborhoods of their adult males, general strikes that paralyzed the little that remained of routine life, the murder of collaborators. Then, gradually, they grew up with promises of change for the better: negotiations, autonomy, independence, work, livelihood. Two of the four carry mobile phones that are never turned off. Fatah activists say that in the GSS[1] interrogation rooms it becomes apparent that a considerable amount of the incriminating evidence against them was gathered by tapping their phones. "Careless amateurism," say members of the generation that did not have cellulars when they were underground some 15 years ago. But all four say they change their phones or numbers daily.

The decision to establish the al-Aqsa Martyrs Brigades came about in phone conversations among Fatah members in every city. It did not come about with an order from above. It is commonly believed that this Fatah military wing was founded in Nablus. But the four members proudly insist that it really started in Tul Karm, although they cannot remember exactly when—days, perhaps weeks after the second Intifada began. "When we saw the Israelis killing so many children in demonstrations," said one, they decided to start using firearms. He was clearly experienced at talking to the press, especially television cameras. He spoke in well-rehearsed, doctrinaire phrases, in a jargon typical of Fatah spokespeople: "The original, fixed goal was to oppose the

1967 occupation. We have no interest in the areas inside the 1948 borders." Adding: "And we actually do have some Jewish friends," from the days when they worked in or around Netanya.

When asked to name an armed action that in their view was "the most successful," they had trouble thinking of one. In their estimate, the Tul Karm al-Aqsa Martyrs Brigade is responsible for killing about 15 settlers. They did not of their own accord mention the murder of two Israeli restaurateurs in Tul Karm on January 23, 2001. When asked, they explain the reason for the murder: revenge for the assassination of Tul Karm's Fatah leader, Dr. Thabet Thabet, on December 31, 2000. Fatah activists say his assassination, by an Israeli firing squad hidden in a truck, as he was leaving his home to go to work as a physician, served as the main impetus to form a military organization in Tul Karm. In other words, if the IDF had intended to undermine the organization, in effect it did exactly the opposite, they say.

"At first, we barely knew how to use a gun," said one, then bragged: "Today, we are expert sharpshooters." The formation of Fatah's military wing was neither organized nor planned, they admit. "Had it been organized, we would have been able to do more to hurt the occupation," said one, giving away their greatest weakness. "We didn't think about what would happen. We didn't think about how things would develop." The Fatah political activists who watched the youths organize as a "military wing," without orders from above, expected a confrontation of two or three months, not more. At first, said one of the four, "each area in which the al-Aqsa Martyrs Brigades were active had it own policy." Now, they maintain, their organization acts according to a centralized, coordinated policy. For example, in order to prevent privately initiated public announcements, seemingly issued by the al-Aqsa Martyrs Brigades every few days, that do not represent the views of the organization, it was decided there would be a single person in the West Bank responsible for making such statements. A special announcement a month ago warned against falsely disseminating leaflets in the West Bank with the signature of this military wing. The absence of a central command, and a single clear address for decision-making in the Fatah, prompts individuals to come out with leaflets of their own, ostensibly on behalf of the movement—for example with threats against particular individuals (as in the case of former minister Nabil `Amar).

It is difficult to know to what extent the overdue decision to centralize the dissemination of leaflets is indeed being implemented. About two weeks ago, leaflets by "al-Aqsa Martyrs" warned the Palestinian Legislative Council not to vote in favor of a no-confidence resolution against the new government formed by Yasser Arafat. These, too, are "forged announcements," says the Fatah. Apparently it's easy to exploit anonymity and send a fax in the name of the intimidating armed youths with a reputation as hotheads.

On January 17, 2002, `Abd al-Salem Hasona of the village of Beit Imrin near Nablus set out from Tul Karm to carry out a terror attack in Hadera. He chose a banquet hall and killed six people celebrating a bat mitzvah. "That was our response to the killing of Raed Karmi" (on January 14th), said the four. "If we started killing Israelis within the 1948 borders, it was only as a response to their tanks and slaughters. No one honored our "security zone," where Palestinian civilians may not be harmed, so why do they expect us to honor the security of Israeli civilians?" The response to the assassination of Karmi, who was "beloved by all," because he managed to slip into settlements, "kill a settler and get out," was particularly difficult "because it was preceded by a period of agreed-upon quiet. That is why all hell broke loose."

Now they have returned to the original policy of attacking only "within the 1967 borders." "But if Israel assassinates any more of our people, we will not honor the green line and we will resume attacks within the 1948 borders." They will not heed Arafat's appeals to not harm civilians. If you are motivated by revenge, they were asked, why does the killing of an armed man elicit a stronger response than the killing of a child by a tank or a semi-automatic rifle? Surprised by the question, they found it difficult to formulate a suitable response. Finally, the youngest member of the group said: "When one of us is killed, we lose a fighter. That is a far greater loss to us than the life of a child, as painful as it may be." Six out of twelve of the founding leaders of the Tul Karm al-Aqsa Martyrs Brigades have been killed to date. The ones Israel has arrested are not the big fish, they say. "Now, new members are joining." They admit, however, that they "were dealt a serious blow." So serious, says A (a senior Fatah activist, former prisoner in Israel, and high-ranking officer in the PA's security apparatus) that they are looking for a way to escape their "heroism." Because they have no idea who is next on Israel's hit list, they adhere even more strongly to a job "that is a few sizes too big for them"—as wanted terrorists, and freedom fighters in their own eyes.

In A's view, they would be happy with an arrangement that would "send them abroad for a couple of years." Says A: "They say, 'We do not like what is happening, we are not bloodthirsty, we want to be free, like other people, why should Israelis be better than us?' and sound no different from thousands of other, unarmed Palestinians." In A's view, and K concurs, they are "nothing." Some, he says, were no more than car thieves. Others have a dubious family history, says D, also a Fatah activist and senior officer in the PA's security apparatus. It is not unusual for criminals of various kinds and those with "dubious family histories" to join the nationalist movements. But how is it that they have succeeded in forcing themselves and their agenda on the entire Fatah movement, and through it, on the entire Palestinian public?

All four admit that there is "fierce competition with Hamas." The Hamas movement is "adept at attacks within the 1948 borders, and we at fighting against the 1967 occupation. It is more important to kill soldiers." A agrees that this competition with Hamas—over political control and grassroots popularity—spurred some political leaders in the Fatah to give free reign to a very small number of guys, who decided to lend the uprising a "military" character. Their numbers grew after Israel's military escalation, and internal competition broke out among Fatah leaders over who could boast the largest number of supporters who fulfill the people's desire to avenge the deaths of Palestinian children and civilians. A thinks that Fatah's Central Committee is to blame for not demonstrating leadership at the beginning of the uprising and not instituting a clear policy for fighting the occupation. K, who does not belong to the Fatah, says that this "mess" is typical of the movement, which elevated to the status of heroes the uprising's youths who barely know how to shoot, and certainly don't know how to plan, and are not authorized to do so.

But M, the host of the four activists for the duration of the interview, says that there was no choice. Someone had to respond to the Israeli army, and the fact that the Israeli army escalated its offensive is unrelated to what the Palestinians did. M was still a little jumpy before the meeting. He took the four youths' weapons and warned them not to harm the Israeli guest. This is indicative not only of the danger the meeting posed, but of the reputation the al-Aqsa Martyrs Brigades have as unpredictable hotheads.

The al-Aqsa Martyrs Brigades in Tul Karm have also killed 15 people suspected of collaborating with Israel. According to their exaggerated figures, they have killed 30. On April 1, 2002, just before the IDF took control of the city, they discovered a group of Palestinian youths being led by the Palestinian police to safe houses and killed them in broad daylight—right in front of bystanders and the police—who did not dare stop them. One of those killed was `Imad al-Hamshari, 23, a father of six. His older brother, a physician, despises the killers. "They are the real collaborators. Within five minutes they killed eight people with Kalashnikovs. They are criminals." In his clinic, between one patient and another, Dr. Muhammad al-Hamshari says that a year-and-a-half ago, his brother was arrested by Jibril Rajoub's Preventative Security. He spent three months in prison and was released "because they didn't have anything on him." But "there is no law here, and two or three months later the General Intelligence Service [headed by Tawfiq Tirawi] arrested him." When they visited `Imad, it was evident that he had been tortured. Sources in the Preventative Security say that the younger al-Hamshari, a mechanic, indeed had contacts with the Israeli GSS, which tried to recruit him when he left for work in Israel. The sources maintain that al-Hamshari told the Preventative Security about this of his own accord, and was arrested.

The Tul Karm al-Aqsa Martyrs Brigade has the dubious honor of being the first to murder women suspected of collaborating. They shot and killed Ahlas Yassin, 35, on August 24, 2002 and her niece Raja `Ali on August 30th. The women's relatives moved away from the neighborhood soon after. Neighbors and activists in women's organizations refused to help track them down. "Do you think we are crazy?" they asked, fearful of retaliation by the armed youths, combined with loathing for collaborators. The four members of the al-Aqsa Martyrs Brigades say Yassin passed on information that led to the assassination of activist Ziad Da `as (and the death of three bystanders). `Ali, they claim, gave out information that led to Karmi's assassination. They have no regrets and do not think that there is anything wrong in their acting as judge, jury, and executioner. "The collaborators do us enormous damage and we have someone in charge of verifying if the accusations are true and whether they warrant execution."

About three weeks ago, one of the more volatile members of the Tul Karm al-Aqsa Martyrs Brigade torched the car of a senior Fatah official. He also sprayed the cars of two of the official's closest friends with bullets. The identity of the perpetrator is known. The case was buried after his father intervened and asked to make peace between the sides and pay for the damage. The presumed reason for the young man's actions was to warn the Fatah official, who recently joined the Preventative Security under its new commander, Zuhair Mansara. One of the Preventative Security's jobs is finding ways to control these hotheads "who have weapons instead of brains." The question of who sent him remains unanswered.

------

1. General Security Services.

October 10, 2002

These are the rules of war as laid down by us every day for the last two years: a Palestinian is a terrorist when he attacks Israeli civilians on both sides of the green line—in Israel and the territories—and when he attacks Israeli soldiers at the entrance to a Palestinian city. A Palestinian is a terrorist when an army unit attacks his neighborhood with tanks and he shoots a soldier who gets out of a tank momentarily, and he is a terrorist when he is hit by helicopter gunfire while holding his rifle. Palestinians are terrorists whether they kill civilians or soldiers.

The Israeli soldier is a fighter when he shoots a missile from a helicopter or a shell from a tank at a group of people gathered in Khan Yunis, after the fighter (or one of his comrades-in-arms) fires a shell or a missile at a house from which the army claims a Qassam rocket was launched and kills a man and woman. He is a fighter when he encounters two armed Palestinians in the brush. The Israeli soldier kills armed people and kills civilians. He kills senior commanders of murderous terrorist cells and he kills kindergarten-aged children and adults in their homes. More accurately: they are killed by IDF fire. Most accurately: they were killed, Palestinian sources claim.

The security authorities and the legal authorities hunt down every single Palestinian terrorist. Hundreds are arrested and inter-rogated to obtain information about a single person. This is a war, but the Palestinians are not arrested as prisoners of war with immunity from interrogation and prosecution. Their names are known, and every detail of the investigations and indictments against them are available to the public and can be published. If and when a flimsy investigation actually identifies an Israeli sol-dier who deviated (killed or used his weapon improperly, looted, or abused people at a checkpoint), his identity remains secret. In hundreds of other cases, the army replies, "we are unfamiliar with the complaint." In thousands of other cases, nobody bothers to query the IDF anymore.

Thousands of Palestinians are held in detention centers. Israel is a lawful state, but it deals them a more severe punishment than denying them their liberty: it denies them family visits before they stand trial.

Dozens of other terrorists have been sentenced to death with-out ever standing trial—they and the civilians in their vicinity. This is called "self-defense by a lawful state attacked by a terror-ist entity." Hundreds of Israelis are involved in these extra-judicial killings and are glorified for it. Palestinians have killed dozens of suspected collaborators without allowing them to stand trial or after kangaroo courts, over the past two years. These are "despi-cable murders carried out by animals living in an entity that does not respect due process and human rights."

Palestinians are expected to obey military orders issued by the State of Israel, as if they were the law of the land. But the state that imposes these orders on the Palestinians, and whose army controls their cities, villages, fields, and water resources, is not responsible for their welfare. It need not treat them as a normal state would, since they are not its citizens and have no voting rights. Nor need it behave like an occupying power, since (in the eyes of the world) the Oslo Accords absolved it of that responsibility when it transferred the administration of more than 90% of the Palestinian population to the Palestinian Authority (PA). The PA became responsible for its citizenry, even when it was denied jurisdiction over most of the territory, and was unable to put down a water pipe without permission from the Israeli Civil Administration. The PA is still responsible for the welfare and safety of the Palestinians, even after its institutions have been bombed and destroyed, and Israeli tanks and helicopters control the entire area, from within and without.

The terrorists position themselves amid the civilian population thereby endangering them and absolving the IDF of responsibility when civilians are killed in their homes. Whereas the fighters, their personal weapons, and their tanks are only guests in the settlements and outposts from which they shoot at the Palestinian civilians—whom the terrorists exploit.

The Palestinians are bloodthirsty and vengeful as indicated by demonstrations and public opinion polls that show Palestinian support for suicide bombings. The Israelis, whom public opinion polls showed supported the assassination of Salah Shehadeh— even if it meant that 14 civilians were killed along with him—are not bloodthirsty and vengeful.

The Palestinian disrupts public order when he violates a curfew imposed by the fighters in the tanks and armored jeeps. Such a Palestinian is punishable: tear gas in the best case, shooting in the worst. The Israeli fighter and his army uphold public order and security when they prevent hundreds of thousands of children from going to school, and teachers from going to work, and patients from going to the hospital, and farmers from going to their fields, and grandmothers from seeing their grandchildren.

Glossary

The '67 territories: territories occupied by Israel in the 1967 war, namely East Jerusalem, the West Bank, the Gaza Strip, and the Golan Heights (the Sinai having since been returned to Egypt.

The 1949 armistice lines: the de facto borders of the State of Israel as delineated in the armistice agreements between Israel and Egypt, Jordan, Syria, and Lebanon in 1949, allotting Israel 79% of the territory of Mandatory Palestine instead of the 55% allotted to the Jewish state in UN resolution 181 which called for the partition of Palestine in 1947.

The borders of June 4, 1967: same territory as the 1949 armistice lines. Israel's de facto internationally recognized (though not acknowledged by Israel as its final) borders. Since the 1967 war (which commenced on June 5th), Israel has maintained military control over 100% of Mandatory Palestine, though its sovereignty has not been extended to the occupied territories (save for the illegal annexation of East Jerusalem in 1967 and the Golan Heights in 1981).

Areas A, B, and C: territorial divisions stipulated in the Oslo accords on the interim agreement for the West Bank (the "Taba Agreement" signed in September 1995, also known as "Oslo II"). Area A denoting full Palestinian civil jurisdiction and internal security control; Area B denoting Palestinian civil jurisdiction and Israeli security control; and Area C denoting full Israeli civil jurisdiction and security control. The territory of each area was to gradually change (A increasing, C decreasing) though the rate and final proportions were never clearly defined. In September 2000, Area C comprised around 60% of the West Bank.

Areas H1 and H2: The two sections of the West Bank city of Hebron as delineated in an agreement signed in January 1997 wherein the Israeli army turned over 80% of the city to the Palestinian Authority (H1), but maintained partial civil and full security control in the Old City of Hebron and its adjacent neighborhoods (H2) where some 450 Jewish settlers and 35,000 Palestinians live.

The green line: popular term for the 1949 armistice line, originally demarcated on the maps in green.

Abu Ali Brigades: military group named for Abu Ali Mustafa, General Secretary of the Popular Front for the Liberation of Palestine (PFLP), assassinated by Israel in August 2001.

Al-Aqsa Intifada: the Palestinian leadership's official name for the popular uprising that erupted after September 28th, 2000, when Ariel Sharon, then Israeli opposition leader, visited Haram al-Sharif (the Temple Mount/Dome of the Rock compound). Seen as a provocation, the Palestinian Authority and Fatah called on the masses to confront Sharon, but only a few dozen officials and activists heeded the call. The next day, Palestinian youths threw stones at Jewish worshippers at the Wailing Wall. The police dispersed the stone-throwers with lethal force, killing four Muslim worshippers and injuring dozens. In response, mass demonstrations broke out throughout the occupied territories and among Palestinian citizens of Israel, and these too were met with escalatory lethal repression by Israeli security forces.

Al-Aqsa Martyrs Brigades: name adopted by Fatah's military cells at the beginning of the second Intifada.

Al-Aqsa Mosque: the mosque marking the place from which Muslims believe the Prophet Muhammad ascended to heaven, constituting the 3rd holiest site in Islam. The compound in which it is situated, known in Arabic as Haram al-Sharif, is believed by Jews to be the site of the Temple.

Al-Bireh: a Palestinian town southwest of Ramallah, population: 30,000.

Al-Damir: Arabic for "conscience," a Palestinian NGO that supports prisoners' rights.

Al-Karmel: Palestinian literary journal founded in Beirut in 1981 by Palestinian poet Mahmoud Darwish, now published in Ramallah.

Al-Risala: the official organ of the Islamic National Salvation Party, an offshoot of Hamas established in Gaza in 1995, which refrains from official involvement in the ideology and practice of armed struggle for "the liberation of all of Palestine."

APC: armored personnel carrier.

Suha Arafat: nee Tawil, Yasser Arafat's wife.

Yasser Arafat: One of the founders of the Fatah movement, Chairperson of the Palestine Liberation Organization (PLO), and Chairperson of the Palestinian Authority (PA).

Ehud Barak: Israeli Chief of Staff under Yitzhak Rabin, Labor Party Prime Minister from 1999-2001.

Bat Shalom: The Jerusalem Women's Action Center, an Israeli NGO.

Bat Yam: Israeli town south of Tel Aviv, population: 140,000.

Bedouin: Arabs who traditionally maintain a semi-nomadic lifestyle and whose main source of livelihood is shepherding.

Yossi Beilin: Minister of Justice under Ehud Barak, one of the Labor Party members to clandestinely initiate the Oslo process with the PLO in 1993.

Beit Daras: a Palestinian village northeast of Gaza occupied and depopulated by Israeli forces in July 1948. All of the village was destroyed. Many of Beit Daras' 2,800 refugees and their descendents now live in Rafah in the southern Gaza Strip.

Beit El: Israeli settlement northeast of Ramallah, population: 4,000.

Beit Hanoun: Palestinian village in the northern Gaza Strip, population: 20,000.

Beit Shemesh: Israeli town west of Jerusalem, population: 40,000.

Beit Sahour: Palestinian town east of Bethlehem, population: 11,000.

Betar Illit: Israeli settlement southwest of Jerusalem, population: 12,000.

Bethlehem: Palestinian town south of Jerusalem, population: 26,000.

Bir Zeit University: Palestinian university located in the village of Bir Zeit, northeast of Ramallah.

B'Tselem: The Israeli Information Center for Human Rights in the Occupied Territories, an Israeli NGO.

Camp David Summit: The failed would-be final stage of negotiations of a final status agreement between Israel and the Palestinians in July-August 2000. President Bill Clinton did not succeed to reconstruct a former Camp David summit, moderated by President Jimmy Carter in 1977, wherein Egypt and Israel negotiated a peace treaty.

Moshe Dayan: Israeli Chief of Staff in the 1956 war, Minister of Defense in the 1967 war. Proponent of the integration of Palestinians into the Israeli economy so as to forestall the realization of their national aspirations.

Democracy and Workers' Rights Center: a Palestinian NGO.

DFLP: the Democratic Front for the Liberation of Palestine; a secular-leftist Palestinian political party.

Dunam: land measurement unit; 1 dunam = 1/4 acre.

Fatah: Arabic acronym (in reverse) for Palestinian Liberation Movement. Founded by Yasser Arafat and other activists in the Palestinian student movement in Kuwait in 1959. Largest mainstream Palestinian political party.

Gaza-Jericho Agreement: signed in May 1994 (also known as "Oslo I"), an agreement stipulating the first stage of Palestinian Authority rule in the Gaza Strip and Jericho enclave.

Gilo: Israeli settlement in southeast Jerusalem considered by Israel to be a "neighborhood" in annexed East Jerusalem.

Baruch Goldstein: American-born Jewish doctor who resided in the settlement of Kiryat `Arba and opened fire on Palestinian worshippers at the Tomb of the Patriarchs / Ibrahimi Mosque in Hebron on February 25, 1994 killing 29 and injuring dozens.

GSS: Israeli General Security Services, also known by its Hebrew acronym as the *Shin Bet* or *Shabak*.

GUPT: General Union of Palestinian Teachers.

Hadash: Hebrew acronym for the Democratic Front for Peace and Equality, a secular-leftist political party composed of the Israeli Communist Party and independent politicians and supported primarily by Palestinian citizens of Israel.

Hadera: Israeli town north of Tel Aviv, population: 70,000.

Hamas: Arabic acronym for the Islamic Resistance Movement. Founded in Gaza in 1988 by leaders of the Palestinian Islamic Brotherhood, which traditionally favored religious missionary work to struggle against the occupation, it was initially tolerated by the Israeli authorities and frowned upon by the Palestinian national movement. Officially, the party calls for armed struggle against Israel and the establishment of an Islamic state in all of Palestine, but has at times hinted that it would accept a temporary "cease fire" with Israel in the form of a Palestinian state in parts of historic Palestine. Not a PLO member, it is seen as the main rival of Yasser Arafat and the Fatah movement.

Hebron: Palestinian town in the southern West Bank. The only Palestinian town with an Israeli settlement in the heart of it, population: 140,000 Palestinians and 500 Jews.

Hizballah: Literally "The Party of God" in Arabic, a Lebanese Shiite Islamic movement backed by Iran. Founded as an umbrella organization for Shiite groups after the Israeli invasion of Lebanon in 1982, it was one of the most active organizations to resist Israel's 18-year occupation of the southern part of the country.

`Id al-Adha: Muslim holiday commemorating Abraham's near sacrifice of his son Ishmael.

`Id al-Fitr: Muslim holiday marking the end of Ramadan.

IDF: Israel Defense Forces.

IMF: International Monetary Fund.

Intifada(s): literally "shaking-off" in Arabic, term used to describe the popular Palestinian uprisings against Israeli occupation begun in 1987 and 2000 respectively.

Islamic Jihad: a movement splintered from the Palestinian Muslim Brotherhood in the mid-1980s that advocates armed struggle for the liberation of Palestine as a prerequisite for Islamic resurgence.

Jabalya: Palestinian refugee camp in the northern Gaza Strip, population: 100,000. (Place with the highest population density in the world).

Jaffa: mixed Arab-Jewish town adjacent to Tel Aviv, which, until the vast majority of its Palestinian residents were expelled in the course of the 1948 war, functioned as an important Palestinian cultural and economic center.

Jenin: Palestinian town in the northern West Bank, population: 31,000, including some 14,000 refugees in the Jenin Refugee Camp.

Ketziot: Hebrew name of a detention camp (also known as "Ansar 3" in Arabic) set up by Israel in the Negev desert during the first Intifada and re-opened in April 2002. In February 2003 it had 1,200 Palestinian inmates, 1,000 of whom were "administrative detainees" — people jailed without due process.

Khan Yunis: Palestinian town in the southern Gaza Strip, population: 105,000, of which at least 60,000 are refugees.

Kiryat `Arba: Israeli settlement northeast of Hebron, population: 8,000.

Knesset: Hebrew name for the Israeli Parliament.

Likud: the rightist-secular governing party in Israel since 1977 (except for short periods of Labor Party rule from 1992-1996 and 1999-2000 and shared power in the form of "national-unity governments" from 1984–1990 and 2001–2002).

Madrid Conference: multilateral Middle East peace negotiations held in 1991–1992 immediately following the 1991 Gulf War. The Palestinian delegation was not allowed to participate as representatives of the PLO and was forced to join the Jordanian delegation instead, though it was appointed by, and openly consulted with, the PLO leadership in Tunis.

MAS: Palestine Economic Policy Research Institute.

Mevaseret Zion: Israeli suburb west of Jerusalem, population: 20,000.

MK: Member of Knesset.

Shaul Mofaz: IDF Chief of Staff under Ehud Barak and Ariel Sharon; appointed Minister of Defense by the latter upon retiring from military service.

MSF: Médecins Sans Frontières (Doctors Without Borders). French humanitarian organization founded in 1972 which offers assistance to populations in distress, victims of natural or man-made disasters, and victims of armed conflict, "without discrimination and irrespective of race, religion, creed or political affiliation."

Nakba Day: literally "catastrophe" in Arabic, Nakba is the Palestinian term for the 1948 war and its aftermath: the dispossession, expulsion, and forced exile of some 750,000 Palestinians and their descendents from their homeland. In 1998 the Palestinian Authority and other Palestinian political organizations called on the people to commemorate Nakba Day on May 15th — the day the State of Israel declared its independence in 1948 according to the Gregorian calendar.

Netzarim: Israeli settlement in the central Gaza Strip, population: 300.

Neve Dekalim: Israeli settlement in the southern Gaza Strip, population: 2,500.

NGO: Non-Governmental Organization.

NIS: New Israeli Shekel, Israel's official currency.

NRP: National Religious Party, a rightist-religious Israeli political party.

Block O: refugee neighborhood in Rafah, adjacent to the Egyptian border.

Old City of Jerusalem: 1 square kilometer of Muslim, Christian, Armenian, and Jewish quarters, surrounded by a wall built by the Ottoman Sultan Suleiman the Magnificent in 1542 and located in the heart of the city. Home to Muslim, Christian, and Jewish holy places, it houses 25 mosques, 65 churches, and 19 synagogues. Population: 33,000, predominantly Palestinian Muslims.

Orient House: PLO headquarters in East Jerusalem, allowed to function as such after the Madrid talks, and shut down by Israeli Prime Minister Ariel Sharon in August 2001.

Oslo Accords: the accords that laid the foundation for the interim agreements between Israel and the PLO, as signed in May 1994 concerning Gaza and Jericho and in September 1995 concerning the West Bank. According to the Oslo Accords, the interim agreements were to be replaced by a final status agreement by May 1999.

PA: Palestinian Authority.

Palestinian People's Party: formerly the Palestinian Communist Party (founded in 1982), which changed its name in 1991.

PCBS: Palestinian Central Bureau of Statistics.

PCHR: Palestinian Center for Human Rights, a Palestinian NGO.

PFLP: Popular Front for the Liberation of Palestine, a secular-leftist Palestinian political party.

PINGO: the umbrella organization of Palestinian NGOs.

PLC: Palestinian Legislative Council.

PLO: Palestine Liberation Organization.

Psagot: Israeli settlement east of Ramallah, population: 1,000.

Qanun (LAW): the Palestinian Society for the Protection of Human Rights and the Environment, a Palestinian NGO.

Quran: The Muslim holy script.

Yitzhak Rabin: Israeli Chief of Staff in the 1967 war, Minister of Defense during the first Intifada, and Labor Party Prime Minister elected in 1992 and assassinated November 4, 1995 by a Jewish rightist-religious activist who sought to halt what he saw as Israel's "surrender" to the Arabs in the form of the Oslo negotiated process.

Ramadan: Muslim holy month of fasting, during which, according to Muslim belief, God granted the Quran to the Prophet Muhammad.

Ramallah: Palestinian town north of Jerusalem. Since the closure imposed on Jerusalem in March 1993, the provisional cultural and political capital of the Palestinian occupied territories, population: 40,000.

Red Crescent Society: Muslim equivalent of the Red Cross.

Ariel Sharon: Israeli Minister of Defense in the 1982 war and Likud Party Prime Minister from 2001-2003, reelected in 2003.

Shas: Israeli political party supported primarily by religious Jews of African/Asian origin.

Sukkoth: Jewish holiday marking the exodus from Egypt, when "the children of Israel" are believed to have lived in huts.

Ta`ayush: Arabic for "coexistence," a joint Jewish-Palestinian Israeli activist group founded with the second Intifada that works in solidarity with Palestinians.

Tanzim: Arabic for "organization." Common name for Fatah's armed wing during the second Intifada; denotes Fatah activists from within the occupied territories as opposed to those who returned from exile in the framework of the Oslo agreements.

Technion: The Israel Institute of Technology.

Tel Aviv: : Israeli city north of Jaffa. Today, Israel's commercial and cultural center, population: 360,000.

Tel Rumeida: the ancient city of Hebron, where Abraham is said to have bargained for the cave he bought to bury his family, and where King David is said to have reigned before moving to Jerusalem. Today, a hill in the city of Hebron inhabited by Palestinians and a handful of Israeli settlers.

Tunnel Riots: massive protests waged by Palestinians in September 1996 that lasted 3 days during which time 1,400 Palestinians were injured, 62 Palestinians were killed, and 15 Israeli soldiers were killed. The protests were provoked by the opening of a tunnel in an Israeli archeological project beneath the Dome of the Rock in the Old City of Jerusalem, linking Via Dolorosa and the Wailing Wall.

Tunnel Road junction: a junction northwest of Bethlehem, leading to a tunnel that connects the settlements of the southern West Bank to Jerusalem, in order to bypass the area's Palestinian communities.

UN: United Nations.

UNDP: United Nations Development Program.

UNRWA: United Nations Relief Works Agency.

Wadi Nar: literally "Valley of Fire" in Arabic, a perilous hilly road east of Jerusalem. Practically the only route connecting the northern and southern parts of the West Bank since entry into Jerusalem was denied to most Palestinians in 1993.

Wailing Wall: Part of the wall built by Herod the Great in 20 BCE to support the esplanade of the Temple in Jerusalem, the site where Jews lament the destruction of the Temple.

Yibne: a Palestinian village southwest of Ramleh occupied and depopulated by Israeli forces in June 1948. Most of the village was destroyed. Many of Yibne's 5,000 refugees and their descendents now live in Rafah in the southern Gaza Strip, in a refugee neighborhood called "Yibne," which has been subject to numerous military attacks and house-demolition campaigns by the Israeli army since the current uprising began.

SEMIOTEXT(E) · NATIVE AGENTS SERIES

Chris Kraus, *Editor*